Gregor Selinka

Three Essays on the Performance Evaluation of Queueing Systems with Time-Dependent Parameters

Bibliografische Information der Deutschen Nationalbibliothek:

Die Deutsche Nationalbibliothek verzeichnet diese Publikation in der Deutschen Nationalbibliografie, detaillierte bibliografische Daten sind im Internet über http://dnb.dnb.de abrufbar.

© 2017 Gregor Selinka

Herstellung und Verlag: BoD – Books on Demand, Norderstedt
Umschlagbild: Hannes Mercker, Mannheim

ISBN: 978-3-74482-297-8

UNIVERSITY OF MANNHEIM

Three Essays on the Performance Evaluation of Queueing Systems with Time-Dependent Parameters

Inauguraldissertation
zur Erlangung des akademischen Grades
eines Doktors der Wirtschaftswissenschaften
der Universität Mannheim

vorgelegt von

Dipl.-Wi.-Ing. Gregor Selinka
Mannheim

Dekan: *Prof. Dr. Dieter Truxius*
Referent: *Prof. Dr. Raik Stolletz*
Korreferent: *Prof. Dr. Cornelia Schön*

Tag der mündlichen Prüfung: *28. Oktober 2016*

Summary

This dissertation consists of three essays dealing with approaches for the non-stationary performance evaluation of queueing systems with time-dependent input parameters. Examples for such systems include time-dependent call volumes and numbers of agents at inbound call centers, non-stationary arrival rates at truck handling facilities, or time-dependent data volumes waiting for transmission in IT communication networks.

The literature survey in the first essay gives a structured overview on methods for the evaluation of single-stage queueing systems with time-dependent but deterministic input parameters. The different approaches are grouped based on their underlying key idea into a new classification scheme that includes the three main categories (i) numerical and analytical solutions, (ii) approaches based on models with piecewise constant parameters, and (iii) approaches based on modified system characteristics. In addition to the description of the approaches and the classification according to the method of analysis, methodological links between different approaches are delineated. The essay concludes with a classification of the literature according to the area of application.

The second and the third essay deal with the development of evaluation approaches for specific queueing systems. In the second essay, a stationary backlog-carryover (SBC) approximation is derived for the performance analysis of a truck handling system at a real-world air cargo terminal. The system includes two heterogeneous truck classes that are handled by two heterogeneous facilities. In order to determine the handling facility to be used, a routing decision has to be made for each truck at its arrival. In a numerical study, the SBC approach is compared to simulation using real-world data.

An inbound call center with impatient customers can be modeled as an $M(t)/M/c + G$ queueing system. The third essay deals with the derivation of an SBC approximation for the non-stationary performance evaluation of such queueing systems. In a numerical study, the new approach is compared to the modified offered load (MOL) approximation and the stationary independent period-by-period (SIPP) approach. The solution of the Chapman-Kolmogorov equations and simulations are used as benchmark. Furthermore, the applicability of the new approach to real-world call center data is shown.

Contents

List of Figures

List of Tables

1 Introduction

Queueing theory provides methodologies for the analysis of waiting lines in stochastic systems that offer services to any kind of customers or jobs. These jobs arrive at the system and are handled by a single server or one of several parallel servers. If all servers are working at the arrival of a job, the job waits until a server becomes available, or is lost if no waiting space is available. Such queueing systems are generally subject to uncertainty as arrival and service processes may include stochastic behavior. A queueing system's performance is evaluated in terms of different performance measures such as the utilization of the servers, the waiting time of a job, or the number of jobs waiting for service. The areas of application of queueing systems are widespread and include the analysis of service systems (e.g. check-in facilities at airports or inbound call centers), manufacturing facilities (e.g. production machines), traffic systems (e.g. signalized road junctions or border checkpoints), and IT systems (e.g. queued documents in cache waiting to be printed).

In real-world, queueing systems are often subject to non-stationarity due to time-dependent input parameters. Using the example of an inbound call center, the arrival and the service process can vary over time. In particular, the arrival pattern of calls often includes several peaks over the course of a day and, additionally, depends on the day of the week. The service process may be time-dependent due to a varying number of active servers based on shift schedules or due to non-stationary service times (e.g. due to different server capabilities or changing service offerings depending on the time of the day).

This dissertation includes three essays on the performance evaluation of queueing systems with deterministic, but time-dependent parameters. In particular, it deals with calculation approaches for the non-stationary behavior in terms of performance measures such as a system's utilization, queue length, and work in process, as well as the waiting and cycle time of a job. The first essay (Chapter 2) incorporates an overview and classification of the existing literature on approaches for the performance evaluation of single-stage queueing systems. The second (Chapter 3) and third essay (Chapter 4) deal with the derivation of approaches for the performance evaluation of one specific setting of a queueing system, respectively.

Chapter 2 gives a structured overview of the existing approaches for the performance evaluation of time-dependent queueing systems. The essay is a joint work together with Justus Arne Schwarz and Raik Stolletz[1]. The survey is restricted to the analysis of single-stage queueing systems with abandonments and retrials, and a waiting room larger or equal to one, i.e., no loss queues without waiting room are considered. Each considered system includes at least one deterministic parameter that changes over time. The different approaches are grouped according to the underlying key idea into the categories: (1) numerical and analytical solutions; (2) approaches based on models with piecewise constant parameters; and (3) approaches based on modified system characteristics. Several subcategories allow for a more detailed classification. For each approach, the description includes an illustration of the underlying key idea, an overview of the related literature, and an explanation of methodological links to other approaches. Even though most of the considered literature is limited to a single method for analysis, some articles include numerical studies that allow for a comparison of several approaches. An overview on these comparative studies is also given in the essay.

---

[1] Schwarz, J. A., G. Selinka, and R. Stolletz (2016): Performance analysis of time-dependent queueing systems: survey and classification. *Omega 63*, 170-189.

In addition to the method-based classification, the work includes a classification of the literature according to the area of application. These areas are extensive and are classified into (1) service systems, (2) road and air traffic systems, as well as (3) IT systems. Here, it is noticeable that approaches based on stationary models are used very often and that some approaches are only used within a specific area of application.

Chapter 3, a joint work together with Axel Franz and Raik Stolletz[2], is dedicated to the performance evaluation of a real-world truck handling system at an air cargo hub. Trucks of two classes (import and export trucks) arrive to the system and are handled at two separate handling facilities 1 and 2. Whereas export shipments can be handled only at facility 1, import shipments can be handled at both facilities. Hence, a routing decision has to be taken for each import truck that depends on the state of the system at the instant of arrival. This truck handling system is modeled by two parallel, single-stage Markovian queueing systems.

With regard to the performance analysis of such a queueing system, a stationary model based on the Chapman-Kolmogorov equations is derived at first. This model is then used within a stationary backlog-carryover approximation based on Stolletz (2008a) that allows for the non-stationary performance evaluation with time-dependent arrival processes. In addition, the approach is able to model routing policies whose decisions depend on the work in process at both handling facilities at the time of a truck's arrival. With respect to the classification scheme introduced in Chapter 2, the derived approximation can be classified as an approach based on stationary models. Within a numerical study, the applicability of the approach to the performance evaluation of stationary queueing systems is shown at first. Secondly, the accuracy of the new approach to the analysis of time-dependent systems is analyzed using artificial data. Thereto, the stationary backlog-carryover approximation is compared to

---

[2] Selinka, G., A. Franz, and R. Stolletz (2014): Time-dependent performance approximation of truck handling operations at an air cargo terminal. *Computers & Operations Research 65*, 164-173.

the simple stationary period-by-period approximation and simulation results are used as benchmark. In the third part of the numerical study, the new approach is applied to the analysis of a real-world truck handling system including real-world arrival and service data. Here, different routing policies are analyzed and a sensitivity analysis is conducted with respect to different system settings of the real-world system.

The joint work together with Raik Stolletz and Thomas I. Maindl[3] in Chapter 4 deals with the analysis of a single-stage queueing system and is motivated by the application in call centers. The considered $M(t)/M/c + G$ queueing system features a time-dependent arrival process and generally distributed abandonments, i.e., jobs leaving the queue before being served due to their personal impatience. There are no restrictions with respect to the distribution of the abandonment times as long as the distribution function is given. Similar to the work given in Chapter 3, a stationary backlog-carryover approach is derived for the non-stationary analysis of such queueing systems. The approach uses the stationary model by Zeltyn and Mandelbaum (2005) as part of its analysis and incorporates an online adjustment of the used interval length in order to improve its accuracy. In addition to the stationary backlog-carryover approximation, the work includes the modified offered load approach introduced by Jagerman (1975) for the analysis of $M(t)/M/c+G$ queueing systems.

The applicability of both approaches to a wide range of system configurations is shown within a numerical study and their approximation quality is compared. These system configurations include systems with different numbers of parallel servers and different levels of abandonments. Furthermore, several distributions of abandonments are considered including Markovian, deterministic, uniformly, and Gamma distributed abandonments. For the case of Markovian abandonments, the solution of the Chapman-Kolmogorov equations is used as benchmark for both ap-

---

[3] Selinka, G., R. Stolletz, and T. I. Maindl (2016): Time-dependent performance analysis of queueing systems with generally distributed abandonments. *Working paper.*

proaches. Otherwise, the approaches are compared to simulation results. In the last part of the numerical study, the stationary backlog-carryover approximation is applied to a real-world call center of a small bank in Israel whose data are provided by the Faculty of Industrial Engineering and Management at the Technion in Haifa (Technion (2000)). Here, the applicability of the stationary backlog-carryover approximation to a system with abandonments that follow an arbitrary distribution given by a distribution function is shown.

The essays in Chapters 2 to 4 can be read independent of each other. Each essay includes an inherent structure including introduction, main part, and conclusion. An overall conclusion and remarks on possible areas for future research are provided in Chapter 5.

2 Performance analysis of time-dependent queueing systems: Survey and classification

Co-authors:

Justus Arne Schwarz and *Raik Stolletz*
Chair of Production Management, Business School, University of
Mannheim, Germany

Published as:

Schwarz, J. A., G. Selinka, and R. Stolletz (2016): Performance analysis
of time-dependent queueing systems: Survey and classification. *Omega*
63, 170-189.

Abstract:

Many queueing systems are subject to time-dependent changes in system parameters, such as the arrival rate or number of servers. Examples
include time-dependent call volumes and agents at inbound call centers,
time-varying air traffic at airports, time-dependent truck arrival rates at
seaports, and cyclic message volumes in computer systems.

There are several approaches for the performance analysis of Queueing
systems with deterministic parameter changes over time. In this survey,
we develop a classification scheme that groups these approaches accord-

ing to their underlying key ideas into (i) numerical and analytical solutions, (ii) approaches based on models with piecewise constant parameters, and (iii) approaches based on modified system characteristics. Additionally, we identify links between the different approaches and provide a survey of applications that are categorized into service, road and air traffic, and IT systems.

2.1 Introduction

Many queueing systems feature time-dependent changes in parameters. Examples of non-stationary parameters, such as the arrival rate or number of servers, include time-dependent call volumes and agents at inbound call centers, time-varying air traffic at airports, non-stationary truck arrival rates at container terminals, and cyclic message volumes in IT systems. Because these time-dependent parameter changes can have a substantial impact on a queueing system's performance, they must be considered in the design and control of such systems.

In this article, we classify performance evaluation methods for single-stage queueing systems with time-dependent but deterministic parameter changes. While such systems are also called non-stationary, time-varying, time-inhomogeneous, or non-homogeneous queueing systems, we solely use the term time-dependent queueing systems.

The analysis of time-dependent queueing systems has a long tradition dating back to Kolmogorov (1931). Since then, the practical relevance of such systems has stimulated increasing interest in various research areas, including mathematics, computer science, and operations management. Such an analysis itself is difficult since common relations for steady-state queueing systems, such as Little's law, must be reformulated (Bertsimas and Mourtzinou (1997)).

The contribution of the present work is a survey and classification of the literature on performance evaluation approaches for time-dependent queueing systems and their applications. Additionally, links between different approaches are identified and discussed.

The remainder of this paper is organized as follows. The scope of the survey and the classification scheme are introduced in Section 2.2. In Section 2.3, approaches for the analytical treatment of time-dependent queueing systems are reviewed and classified according to the developed scheme. A visualization of links between the approaches and a review of numerical studies that compare several methods are provided in Section 2.4. Areas of application and their unique characteristics are described in Section 2.5. In Section 2.6, concluding remarks and areas for future research are provided.

2.2 Scope and classification scheme

The survey presented in this paper reviews and classifies approaches for the time-dependent performance evaluation of single-stage queueing systems without spatial dimension, known as point queues, that include

- abandonments and retrials,

- arrivals from an infinite population that are served individually by a single server or one of multiple parallel servers (for a treatment of finite source systems, see e.g. Alfa (1979), Chung and Min (2014), and references within),

- waiting rooms larger or equal to one (i.e., waiting or loss-waiting systems; for a recent but incomplete survey of time-dependent loss queues, see Alnowibet and Perros (2006)),

- and deterministic system parameters that change over time (the transient analysis of systems with constant parameters is addressed, e.g., by Van de Coevering (1995), Tarabia (2000), and references within).

We survey approaches that allow for the performance analysis of arbitrary time instances. Discrete-event simulation is also applied for time-dependent performance evaluation. However, it is associated with a simulation error. This error can be reduced by an increase in the number of replications at the price of increasing run times (Nasr and Taaffe (2013)). Moreover, structural system properties remain intractable. Thus, the survey comprises only approaches which do not require the generation of random numbers.

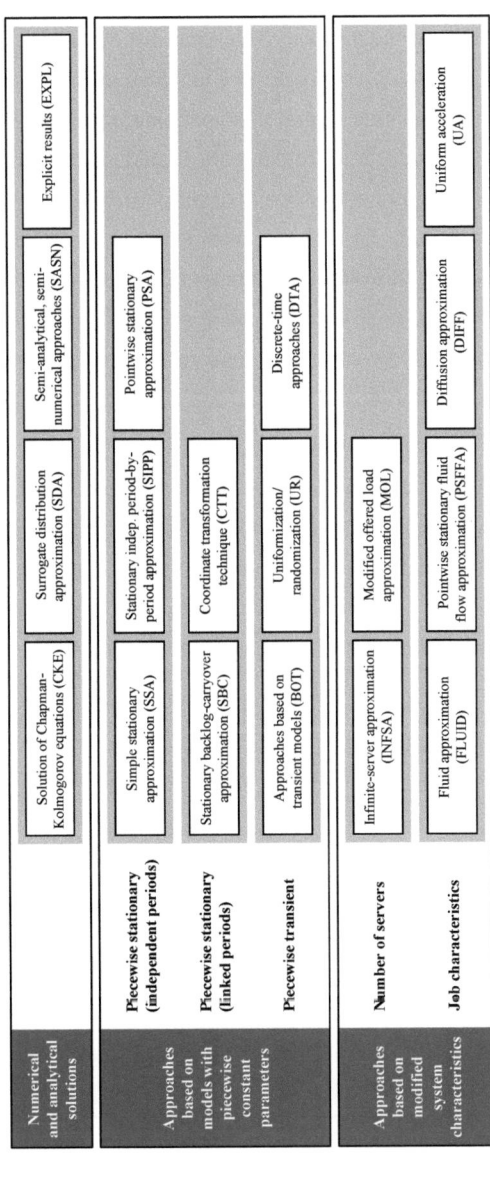

Figure 2.1: Classification of approaches

We identify three main categories of evaluation approaches: the first category comprises numerical and analytical solution approaches for systems of equations that describe the time-dependent behavior of a queueing system (Section 2.3.1); the second category includes approaches that assume piecewise constant parameters and that apply stationary or transient models (Section 2.3.2); and the third category includes approximation methods that modify the number of servers or properties of the processed jobs (Section 2.3.3). Figure 2.1 presents our classification scheme including these categories and all evaluation approaches reviewed in this work. In the corresponding sections, each approach is described in terms of its key idea, its chronological development, and its advantages and limitations. These descriptions include only references that develop or methodologically extend an approach.

All surveyed references together with the characteristics of the analyzed queueing systems are listed in Tables 2.2, 2.3, and 2.5 to 2.10. For each reference that considers several queueing systems, the characteristics of the most general one are given. The references are sorted chronologically for each approach. The notation used in the following sections is provided in Table 2.1.

Table 2.1: Notation

Model description

λ	Arrival rate
X	Arriving batch size distribution
c	Number of parallel servers
μ	Processing rate
Y	Batch service size distribution
s	Max. no. of jobs served by a batch server
$\rho = \frac{\lambda}{c\mu}$	Traffic intensity
K	Maximum no. of jobs in the system
PPrio	Preemptive priority
NPPrio	Non-preemptive priority
t	Time parameter
$(\cdot)'$	Derivatives with respect to time

Performance measures

U	Utilization
L^Q	No. of jobs in the queue
L^S	No. of jobs in the system

Table 2.1: cont.

W^Q	Waiting time of a job
W^S	Sojourn time of a job

Probabilities

$P_n = P(L^S = n)$	Probability of n jobs in the system
$P_w = P(W^Q > 0)$	Probability of waiting
$\mathbf{P} = (P_0, P_1, ...)$	Vector of state probabilities

The development of approaches for the performance evaluation is often driven by real-world problems. Hence, many articles include both, an evaluation approach and its application to a real-world problem. The classification according to the area of application considers the references that include a detailed description of a specific application accompanied by a numerical study. The reviewed applications of the approaches are divided into the areas of service systems (Section 2.5.1), road and air traffic systems (Section 2.5.2), and IT systems (Section 2.5.3).

2.3 Performance evaluation approaches

2.3.1 Numerical and analytical solutions

The **Chapman-Kolmogorov equations (CKEs)** compose a set of differential equations (DEs) that describes the dynamic behavior of a Markovian queueing system. For an $M(t)/M(t)/c$ system, the DEs are given as

$$P'_0(t) = \mu(t) \cdot P_1(t) - \lambda(t) \cdot P_0(t), \qquad n = 0,$$
$$P'_n(t) = (n+1) \cdot \mu(t) \cdot P_{n+1}(t) + \lambda(t) \cdot P_{n-1}(t)$$
$$- (\lambda(t) + n \cdot \mu(t)) \cdot P_n(t), \qquad 1 \le n < c, \quad (2.1)$$
$$P'_n(t) = c \cdot \mu(t) \cdot P_{n+1}(t) + \lambda(t) \cdot P_{n-1}(t)$$
$$- (\lambda(t) + c \cdot \mu(t)) \cdot P_n(t), \qquad n \ge c.$$

Analytical solutions for these DEs exist only for special cases, e.g., $c = \infty$. However, solutions can be obtained numerically by using the Euler method or a Runge Kutta scheme. Systems with an infinite waiting room result in an infinite number of DEs. Kolesar et al. (1975) suggest approximating such systems by using a system with a finite but sufficiently large waiting room.

The CKEs are introduced by Kolmogorov (1931) for an $M(t)/M/c$ system. The numerical solution of the CKEs is used for the performance evaluation of an $M(t)/M/1/K$ system by Koopman (1972), an $M(t)/M(t)/1/K$ system with two separate queues and a common server by Bookbinder (1986), and a multi-class $M(t)/M(t)/1/K/$NPPrio system by Van As (1986). In addition, the numerical solution is used in the evaluation part of optimization algorithms, e.g., by Parlar (1984) and Nozari (1985), as well as in the dynamic programming approaches of Bookbinder and Martell (1979) and Jung and Lee (1989b).

The numerical solution for the CKEs has the advantage that the complete time-dependent distribution of the state probabilities is obtained. Thus, this solution can be used to calculate relevant quantiles (Ingolfsson et al. (2002)). However, the main disadvantages are that the solution approach applies only to Markovian systems and has long computation times (Ingolfsson et al. (2007)).

Approximation approaches are proposed to reduce computation times. Instead of solving the CKEs directly, Escobar et al. (2002) suggest first reducing the state space of an $M(t)/E_k(t)/c/K$ system as an approximation of the original state space and then solving the reduced number of DEs numerically.

Another widely used approach for reducing the computational effort is the **closure approximation** or **surrogate distribution approximation (SDA)**. In this approach, the large or infinite number of CKEs is replaced by a small number of DEs for the moments of the distribution of the number of jobs in the system. The k-th moment differential equation (MDE) is obtained by summation of the differential equations in (2.1), each multiplied by n^k. The differential equations for the first moment $\mathrm{E}[L^S(t)]$ and the variance $\mathrm{Var}[L^S(t)]$ of an $M(t)/M(t)/c$ system are given by

$$\mathrm{E}[L^S(t)]' = \sum_{n=0}^{\infty} n \cdot P'_n(t)$$

$$= \lambda(t) - c \cdot \mu(t) + \mu(t) \cdot \sum_{n=0}^{c-1} (c - n) \cdot P_n(t), \quad (2.2)$$

$$\mathrm{Var}[L^S(t)]' = \sum_{n=0}^{\infty} \left(n - \mathrm{E}[L^S(t)]\right)^2 \cdot P'_n(t)$$

$$= \sum_{n=0}^{\infty} n^2 \cdot P'_n(t) - 2 \cdot \mathrm{E}[L^S(t)] \cdot \sum_{n=0}^{\infty} n \cdot P'_n(t)$$

$$= \lambda(t) + c \cdot \mu(t) - \mu(t) \cdot \sum_{n=0}^{c-1} (c - n) \cdot P_n(t)$$

$$\cdot \left(2 \cdot \mathrm{E}[L^S(t)] + 1 - 2 \cdot n\right). \quad (2.3)$$

MDEs (2.2) and (2.3) are independent of the maximum number of jobs in the system. Hence, systems with a large or infinite waiting room can be analyzed efficiently. However, to solve these MDEs, the time-dependent state probabilities $P_n(t)$ must be known. They are assumed to follow a certain distribution that *closes* the set of MDEs. This *surrogate distribution* is always chosen such that its first and second moments match $\mathrm{E}[L^S(t)]$ and $\mathrm{Var}[L^S(t)]$, respectively. The closed MDEs can then be solved numerically.

The idea of focusing on the analysis of MDEs is used in an earlier study by Clarke (1956). However, Rider (1976) reports the first attempt to approximate the expected queue length of an $M(t)/M(t)/1$ system with a closure for the probability of an idling server. Since then, different types of distributions have been used as a surrogate distribution. For instance,

15

Rothkopf and Oren (1979) use the negative binomial distribution for the number of jobs in an $M(t)/M(t)/c$ system. Clark (1981) shows that the Polya Eggenberger distribution yields superior results for the same type of system. The Polya Eggenberger distribution is also used for priority queues by Taaffe and Clark (1988) and phase-type arrival and service processes by Ong and Taaffe (1988). These models go along with an increased state space. Taaffe and Ong (1987) introduce state-space partitioning to handle the growing state space. Instead of using a single SDA for the complete state space, the approximation quality is improved by introducing subspaces and allowing for different surrogate distributions depending on the respective subspaces. Lau and Song (2008) analyze a queue with multiple job classes by first aggregating the classes, then applying the model of Rothkopf and Oren (1979), and subsequently disaggregating the results again. Pender (2014a) uses the Poisson distribution as a surrogate distribution and obtains a closed-form solution for $E[L^S(t)]$. To improve the quality of the approximation of $Var[L^S(t)]$, he suggests a truncated Poisson-Charlier polynomial expansion. In an approach unlike the other approaches, Massey and Pender (2013) propose using a continuous distribution for the approximation of the queueing process. Thereby, they derive the so-called Gaussian-variance and Gaussian-skewness approximations. These approaches are complemented by the approach of Pender (2014b), who includes the fourth MDE, reflecting the kurtosis of the queue length distribution, in his approximation based on a Gram Charlier expansion.

A key idea of the SDA is to calculate only moments of a distribution. Thus, the performance analysis is limited to these moments. Typically, the first and second moments of the number of jobs in the system are calculated. The SDA requires the Markov property for the arrival and service process. However, the use of phase-type distributions allows for the analysis of different coefficients of variations (Taaffe and Clark (1988)). This comes at the cost of an increased, but still limited, number of DEs (Ong and Taaffe (1988)).

Markovian queueing systems are often described by generating functions that can often be reduced to an integral equation or formulations that include modified Bessel functions. These evaluation approaches are known as **semi-analytical, semi-numerical (SASN)** approaches (Tan et al. (2013)). A survey and numerical comparison of early SASN approaches is provided by Leese and Boyd (1966).

Clarke (1956) obtains a Volterra-type integral equation for the probability of an empty system in an $M(t)/M(t)/1$ system. An explicit solution is found for the special case of a constant relation $\lambda(t)/\mu(t)$. The approaches of Luchak (1956) and Luchak (1957) involve Taylor expansions to obtain the probability of jobs in the system and the busy period of an $M(t)/PH(t)/1$ system, respectively. Rosenlund (1976) studies the busy period of an $M(t)^X/G/1$ system with batch arrivals distributed according to X. The system also features balking, i.e., arriving jobs join the queue only with a certain probability. Lyubarskii (1982) obtains the busy period of a $G(t)/G(t)/1$ system as a two-dimensional Volterra integral equation. Wragg (1963) and Zhang and Coyle (1991) find the complete state probability distribution of an $M(t)/M(t)/1$ system as a solution of integral equations. Stadje (1990) develops a solution approach for the $M(t)/M(t)/2$ system that is similar to the approach of Clarke (1956). A multi-server $M(t)/M(t)/c$ system is analyzed by Margolius (1999). Margolius (2005) derives integral equations for the probability distribution of jobs in an $M(t)/M(t)/c(t)$ system. By considering quasi-birth-and-death processes, Margolius (2007) generalizes her results to phase-type distributions and establishes a connection with matrix analytic methods (Margolius (2008)). Al-Seedy et al. (2009) extend the analysis of $M(t)/M(t)/1$ systems by incorporating time-dependent balking. For a special structure of $\lambda(t)$ and $\mu(t)$, Al-Seedy and Al-Ibraheem (2003) and El-Sherbiny (2010) obtain the probability distribution of $L^S(t)$ in an $M(t)/M(t)/\infty$ system.

Nelson and Taaffe (2004) derive a quasi-closed form of MDEs that describes the expected number $E[L^S(t)]$ and the variance $Var[L^S(t)]$ of jobs in the system in a $PH(t)/PH(t)/\infty$ system and integrate them numerically. Similarly, Nasr and Taaffe (2013) derive quasi-closed MDEs for the first and second moments of the departure process of a $PH(t)/M(t)/c/K$ system. In contrast to the SDA, the partial-moment differential equations that are used to close the MDEs are exact.

Table 2.2 summarizes the references that use a numerical solution approach and links them to the considered queueing systems. It becomes apparent that the approaches are applicable to a wide range of queueing systems with features such as priorities and abandonments. However, the numerical solutions of the CKEs and the SDA exploit the Markovian property. Notably, Czachórski et al. (2009) use the CKE approach only for the special case of exponential distributions, and Rothkopf and Johnston (1982) analyze an $M(t)/M/1$ system and then scale the results according to the Polaczek-Kintchine formula to integrate general service times.

Table 2.2: Numerical solution approaches

Reference	Queueing system							
Numerical solution of the CKEs								
Kolmogorov (1931)	$M(t)$	/	M	/	c			
Leese and Boyd (1966)	$M(t)$	/	M	/	1			
Koopman (1972)	$M(t)$	/	M	/	1	/	K	
Kolesar et al. (1975)	$M(t)$	/	$M(t)$	/	$c(t)$			
Rider (1976)	$M(t)$	/	$M(t)$	/	1			
Bookbinder and Martell (1979)	$M(t)$	/	M	/	c	/	K	
Rothkopf and Oren (1979)	$M(t)$	/	$M(t)$	/	c			
Clark (1981)	$M(t)$	/	$M(t)$	/	c			
Parlar (1984)	$M(t)$	/	$M(t)$	/	c	/	K	
Nozari (1985)	$M(t)$	/	M	/	c			
Bookbinder (1986)	$M(t)$	/	$M(t)$	/	1	/	K	
Van As (1986)	$M(t)$	/	M	/	1	/	K	/ NPPrio
Taaffe and Ong (1987)	$PH(t)$	/	$M(t)$	/	c	/	K	
Ong and Taaffe (1988)	$PH(t)$	/	$PH(t)$	/	1	/	K	
Taaffe and Clark (1988)	$M(t)$	/	$M(t)$	/	1	/	K	/ NPPrio
Jung and Lee (1989b)	$M(t)$	/	M	/	$c(t)$			
Tipper and Sundareshan (1990)	$M(t)$	/	M	/	1			
Green and Kolesar (1991)	$M(t)$	/	M	/	c			
Green et al. (1991)	$M(t)$	/	M	/	c			
Jung (1993)	$M(t)$	/	M	/	c			
Green and Kolesar (1995)	$M(t)$	/	M	/	c			
Green and Kolesar (1997)	$M(t)$	/	M	/	c			
Massey and Whitt (1997)	$M(t)$	/	M	/	c			

Reference	Queueing system						
Escobar et al. (2002)	$M(t)$	/	$E_k(t)$	/	c	/	K
Ingolfsson et al. (2002)	$M(t)$	/	M	/	$c(t)$	/	K
Ingolfsson et al. (2007)	$M(t)$	/	M	/	$c(t)$		
Czachórski et al. (2009)	$G(t)$	/	G	/	1	/	K / PPrio
Gillard and Knight (2014)	$M(t)$	/	M	/	$c(t)$		
Jacquillat and Odoni (2015)	$M(t)$	/	$E_k(t)$	/	1		

Surrogate distribution approximation

Reference	Queueing system						
Rider (1976)	$M(t)$	/	$M(t)$	/	1		
Rothkopf and Oren (1979)	$M(t)$	/	$M(t)$	/	c		
Clark (1981)	$M(t)$	/	$M(t)$	/	c		
Rothkopf and Johnston (1982)	$M(t)$	/	G	/	1		
Taaffe and Ong (1987)	$PH(t)$	/	$M(t)$	/	c	/	K
Ong and Taaffe (1988)	$PH(t)$	/	$PH(t)$	/	1	/	K
Taaffe and Clark (1988)	$M(t)$	/	$M(t)$	/	1	/	K / NPPrio
Ingolfsson et al. (2007)	$M(t)$	/	M	/	$c(t)$		
Lau and Song (2008)	$M(t)$	/	M	/	c		
Massey and Pender (2013)	$M(t)$	/	M	/	$c(t)$		$+M$
Pender (2014a)	$M(t)$	/	$M(t)$	/	$c(t)$		$+M(t)$
Pender (2014b)	$M(t)$	/	$M(t)$	/	$c(t)$		$+M(t)$

Semi-analytical, semi-numerical approaches

Reference	Queueing system						
Clarke (1956)	$M(t)$	/	$M(t)$	/	1		
Luchak (1956)	$M(t)$	/	$PH(t)$	/	1		
Luchak (1957)	$M(t)$	/	$PH(t)$	/	1		
Wragg (1963)	$M(t)$	/	$M(t)$	/	1		
Leese and Boyd (1966)	$M(t)$	/	M	/	1		
Rosenlund (1976)	$M(t)^X$	/	G	/	1		
Lyubarskii (1982)	$G(t)$	/	$G(t)$	/	1		
Stadje (1990)	$M(t)$	/	$M(t)$	/	2		
Zhang and Coyle (1991)	$M(t)$	/	$M(t)$	/	1		
Margolius (1999)	$M(t)$	/	$M(t)$	/	c		
Al-Seedy and Al-Ibraheem (2003)	$M(t)$	/	$M(t)$	/	∞		
Nelson and Taaffe (2004)	$PH(t)$	/	$PH(t)$	/	∞		
Margolius (2005)	$M(t)$	/	$M(t)$	/	c		
	$M(t)$	/	M	/	$c(t)$		
Margolius (2007)	$PH(t)$	/	$M(t)$	/	1		
Margolius (2008)	$M(t)$	/	E_k	/	1		
	$M(t)$	/	$M(t)$	/	1		
Al-Seedy et al. (2009)	$M(t)$	/	$M(t)$	/	1		
El-Sherbiny (2010)	$M(t)$	/	$M(t)$	/	∞		
Nasr and Taaffe (2013)	$PH(t)$	/	$M(t)$	/	c	/	K

Analytical results and explicit solutions (EXPL) for time-dependent queueing systems exist only for special system configurations and usually cannot be generalized.

Palm (1943) and Khintchine (1969) show that in an $M(t)/M/\infty$ system, the number of jobs $L^S(t)$ is Poisson distributed for a queueing system which started operating in the distant past. Newell (1966) extends the results to general service times. Ramakrishnan (1980) provides a simple argument for these findings for the special case of deterministic service times. Sharma and Gupta (1983) consider an $M(t)/PH/\infty$ system and prove that $L^S(t)$ is Poisson distributed if it follows a Poisson distribution at the beginning of the time horizon. For exponentially distributed service times and a given number of jobs at $t = 0$, Thakur et al. (1972) derive the mean and variance of $L^S(t)$. Abol'nikov (1968) obtains the generating function for the number of jobs in an $M(t)^X/M/\infty$ system and uses it to derive $E[L^S(t)]$. Shanbhag (1966) studies an $M(t)^X/G/\infty$ system and confirms that $L^S(t)$ is a Poisson process for the special case of an initially empty system and $P(X = 1) = 1$, i.e., all jobs arrive individually. Carrillo (1991) and Eick et al. (1993b) review reported analytical results with respect to the $M(t)/G/\infty$ system. In addition, Eick et al. (1993b) highlight that in contrast to the stationary case, $L^S(t)$ depends on the service time distribution beyond its mean.

Brown and Ross (1969), Purdue (1974a), and Purdue (1974b) extend the analysis to time-dependent service time distributions. Brown and Ross (1969) show that for the $M(t)^{X(t)}/G(t)/\infty$ system, $L^S(t)$ and the number of departures $D^{S,c}(t)$ up to time t follow a compound Poisson process. Purdue (1974b) and Foley (1982) demonstrate that $L^S(t)$ and $D^{S,c}(t)$ correspond to Poisson processes if the system is initially empty and if batch arrivals are omitted. McCalla and Whitt (2002) derive an explicit formula for $E[L^S(t)]$ in a $G(t)^{X(t)}/G(t)/\infty$ system and propose an approximation for the distribution of $L^S(t)$, since it is not a Poisson distribution.

Several authors focus on the analysis of the $M(t)/M(t)/\infty$ system. Purdue (1974a) obtains the mean and variance of $L^S(t)$, given the initial distribution of jobs $L^S(0)$. For the special case of an initially empty or Poisson-distributed number of jobs in the system, Collings and Stoneman

(1976) confirm that $L^S(t)$ is Poisson distributed. Additionally, Kambo and Bhalaik (1979) obtain the joint probability distribution of $L^S(t)$ and $D^{S,c}(t)$, which is used to derive the time-dependent mean and variance of both $L^S(t)$ and $D^{S,c}(t)$. Seemingly unaware of the previous findings, Ellis (2010) derives the same formulas for $E[L^S(t)]$ and $\text{Var}[L^S(t)]$ as obtained earlier by Kambo and Bhalaik (1979). Both Ellis (2010) and Kambo and Bhalaik (1979) demonstrate that the expected number of jobs in the system can be described by DE (2.4) with solution (2.5)

$$E[L^S(t)]' = \lambda(t) - \mu(t) \cdot E[L^S(t)], \qquad (2.4)$$

$$E[L^S(t)] = E[L^S(0)] \cdot e^{-\int_0^t \mu(\tau)d\tau}$$
$$+ e^{-\int_0^t \mu(\tau)d\tau} \cdot \int_0^t \lambda(\tau) e^{\int_0^\tau \mu(r)dr} d\tau. \qquad (2.5)$$

Thakur and Rescigno (1978) establish that solution (2.5) for a stochastic system is equivalent to the solution for a $D(t)/D(t)/\infty$ system.

Dai (1998) derives bounds on the moment-generating function of $L^S(t)$ for an $M(t)/M(t)/1$ system and discusses bounds on $E[L^S(t)]$. Knessl and Yang (2002) obtain explicit results for an $M(t)/M(t)/1$ system given a special form of the traffic intensity. Green and Soares (2007) find exact formulas for the probability $P(W^Q(t) > w)$ of waiting longer than w time units in an $M(t)/M/c(t)$ system under the assumption that the state probabilities $P_n(t)$ are known and that a maximum of one change in the number of servers occurs in the interval under consideration. For the case of more than one change, they propose approximation formulas. Kim and Ha (2012) exploit the property that the explicit solution for an $M(t)/M/\infty$ system can be used to model an $M(t)/M/c(t) + M$ system with Poisson abandonments if the abandonment rate equals the service rate.

Except for four references in Table 2.3, all the references report results for infinite-server systems. In addition, all but one of the analyzed queueing systems share the property of a Poisson arrival process with time-dependent rate.

Table 2.3: Analytical results and explicit solutions

Reference	Queueing system			
Palm (1943)	$M(t)$	/ M	/ ∞	
Newell (1966)	$M(t)$	/ G	/ ∞	
Shanbhag (1966)	$M(t)^X$	/ G	/ ∞	
Abol'nikov (1968)	$M(t)^X$	/ M	/ ∞	
Brown and Ross (1969)	$M(t)^{X(t)}$	/ $G(t)$	/ ∞	
Khintchine (1969)	$M(t)$	/ M	/ ∞	
Thakur et al. (1972)	$M(t)$	/ M	/ ∞	
Purdue (1974a)	$M(t)$	/ $M(t)$	/ ∞	
Purdue (1974b)	$M(t)$	/ $G(t)$	/ ∞	
Collings and Stoneman (1976)	$M(t)$	/ $M(t)$	/ ∞	
Thakur and Rescigno (1978)	$M(t)$	/ $M(t)$	/ ∞	
Kambo and Bhalaik (1979)	$M(t)$	/ $M(t)$	/ ∞	
Ramakrishnan (1980)	$M(t)$	/ D	/ ∞	
Foley (1982)	$M(t)$	/ $G(t)$	/ ∞	
Sharma and Gupta (1983)	$M(t)$	/ $PH(t)$	/ ∞	
Eick et al. (1993a)	$M(t)$	/ G	/ ∞	
Eick et al. (1993b)	$M(t)$	/ G	/ ∞	
Dai (1998)	$M(t)$	/ $M(t)$	/ 1	
Green and Kolesar (1998)	$M(t)$	/ G	/ ∞	
Knessl and Yang (2002)	$M(t)$	/ $M(t)$	/ 1	
McCalla and Whitt (2002)	$G(t)^{X(t)}$	/ $G(t)$	/ ∞	
Buczkowski and Kulkarni (2006)	$M(t)$	/ G	/ ∞	
Green and Soares (2007)	$M(t)$	/ M	/ $c(t)$	
Ellis (2010)	$M(t)$	/ $M(t)$	/ ∞	
Kuraya et al. (2011)	$M(t)$	/ M	/ ∞	
Kim and Ha (2012)	$M(t)$	/ M	/ $c(t)$	$+M$

2.3.2 Approaches based on models with piecewise constant parameters

2.3.2.1 Piecewise stationary models with independent periods

This set of approaches divides the overall time horizon T into intervals for which constant input parameters are assumed. The performance in each interval $[a_i, b_i]$ ($i = 1, 2, ..., I$) is then analyzed independently by using steady-state formulas. The approaches differ in the length l of the analyzed intervals and the determination of the input parameters in the corresponding performance calculations (see Table 2.4 for the case of a time-dependent arrival rate $\lambda(t)$).

Table 2.4: Performance evaluation methods based on piecewise stationary models

Method	Input in performance evaluation
Interval length: $l = T$ ($t \in [0, T]$)	
SSA Green et al. (1991)	$\tilde{\lambda}(i) = \frac{1}{T} \int\limits_{0}^{T} \lambda(t)\,dt$
SPEA Green and Kolesar (1995)	$\tilde{\lambda}(i) = \max\limits_{t \in [0, T]} \lambda(t)$
SPHA Green and Kolesar (1995)	$\tilde{\lambda}(i) = \frac{1}{b-a} \int\limits_{a}^{b} \lambda(t)\,dt$ with peak interval $[a, b]$
Interval length: $0 < l < T$ ($t \in [a_i, b_i]$)	
SIPP Avg Kolesar et al. (1975)	$\tilde{\lambda}(i) = \frac{1}{l} \int\limits_{a_i}^{b_i} \lambda(t)\,dt$
SIPP Max Green et al. (2001)	$\tilde{\lambda}(i) = \max\limits_{t \in [a_i, b_i]} \lambda(t)$
SIPP Mix Green et al. (2001)	$\tilde{\lambda}(i) = \begin{cases} \frac{1}{l} \int\limits_{a_i}^{b_i} \lambda(t)\,dt, & \text{if } \frac{d\lambda(t)}{dt} > 0 \ \forall t \in [a_i, b_i] \\ \max\limits_{t \in [a_i, b_i]} \lambda(t), & \text{otherwise} \end{cases}$
Lag Avg Green et al. (2001)	$\tilde{\lambda}(i) = \frac{1}{l} \int\limits_{a_i - \frac{1}{\mu}}^{b_i - \frac{1}{\mu}} \lambda(t)\,dt$
Lag Max Green et al. (2001)	$\tilde{\lambda}(i) = \max\limits_{t \in [a_i - \frac{1}{\mu}, b_i - \frac{1}{\mu}]} \lambda(t)$
Lag Mix Green et al. (2001)	$\tilde{\lambda}(i) = \begin{cases} \frac{1}{l} \int\limits_{a_i - \frac{1}{\mu}}^{b_i - \frac{1}{\mu}} \lambda(t)\,dt, & \text{if } \frac{d\lambda(t)}{dt} > 0 \ \forall t \in [a_i - \frac{1}{\mu}, b_i - \frac{1}{\mu}] \\ \max\limits_{t \in [a_i - \frac{1}{\mu}, b_i - \frac{1}{\mu}]} \lambda(t), & \text{otherwise} \end{cases}$
Interval length: $l = 0$ ($t = a_i = b_i$)	
PSA Newell (1979)	$\tilde{\lambda}(i) = \lambda(t)$
Lagged PSA Green and Kolesar (1997)	$\tilde{\lambda}(i) = \lambda(t - \frac{1}{\mu})$
ASA Whitt (1991)	$\tilde{\lambda}(i) = \mu \int\limits_{t - \frac{1}{\mu}}^{t} \lambda(\tau)\,d\tau$

23

Table 2.4: cont.

Method	Input in performance evaluation
EAA Thompson (1993)	$\tilde{\lambda}(i) = \mu \int\limits_{t-\frac{1}{\mu}-\mathrm{E}[W^Q]}^{t-\mathrm{E}[W^Q]} \lambda(\tau)d\tau$
RA Pang and Whitt (2012b)	$\tilde{\lambda}(i) = \int\limits_{0}^{\infty} \lambda(t-\tau)\delta e^{-\delta\tau}d\tau$

The **simple stationary approximation (SSA)** averages the system parameters over the complete time horizon. Green et al. (1991) apply this approach to systems with periodic time-dependent input parameters. The *simple peak epoch approximation (SPEA)* approximates the time-dependent performance based on the stationary performance by using the instantaneous peak input parameters. In a similar way, the *simple peak hour approximation (SPHA)* divides the time horizon into intervals and uses the input parameters of the peak interval as inputs in the performance calculation. Both concepts are used by Green and Kolesar (1995) for an $M(t)/M/c$ system and by Green and Kolesar (1998) for an $M(t)/M/\infty$ system, each with a periodic input arrival rate.

Shorter intervals are used by the **stationary independent period-by-period approximation (SIPP)**. Therein, the *SIPP Avg* considers the average over an interval; the *SIPP Max*, the maximum; and the *SIPP Mix*, a combination of the mean and maximum as inputs in the performance calculations. The lagged versions of the SIPP incorporate a time lag of one expected service time between the input parameters and the resulting system performance.

The interval length is set to $l = 0$ in the **pointwise stationary approximation (PSA)**. Here, the instantaneous parameter values serve as inputs in the performance calculation. Similar to the Lag SIPP, the *Lagged PSA* considers a time lag between the input parameters and the resulting performance values. The *average stationary approximation (ASA)* uses the mean value over the preceding interval $[t-\frac{1}{\mu}, t]$ as the input in the performance calculation at time t. In the similar *effective arrival rate approxi-*

mation (EAA), the considered interval of input parameters is additionally shifted backward in time by the expected waiting time. The *recent approximation (RA)* calculates a weighted average of the parameters up to time t with weight factor δ. This approach is applied to infinite-server queues with dependencies among successive service times indicated by superscript D in the Kendall notation (Pang and Whitt (2012a)). A peak epoch analysis of a periodic $M(t)/M/c$ system is performed by Green and Kolesar (1997) with a *lagged PSA*, which considers the difference between the time of the peak value of the probability of delay when the standard PSA is applied and the time of the real peak value.

The main advantage of the approaches described in this subsection is their low computational complexity, especially when closed-form steady-state solutions exist for the considered system configuration (Ingolfsson et al. (2007)). However, any transient behavior within an evaluation interval is neglected, which results in approximation errors, especially for highly utilized systems in which long transient phases occur until the steady state is reached (Green and Kolesar (1991)). Further approximation errors result from the independent analysis of consecutive intervals, as a high number of waiting jobs at the end of one interval, e.g., has a substantial impact on the expected waiting time in the subsequent interval. The approaches cannot be used for the analysis of overloaded systems if no steady state exists (Jiménez and Koole (2004)). Whitt (1991) shows that the PSA is asymptotically correct for an $M(t)/M(t)/c$ system if the arrival and service rates increase with constant traffic intensity (compare with uniform acceleration in Section 2.3.3.2). The accuracy of the PSA for an $M(t)/M/c$ system with and without abandonments is analyzed by Steckley and Henderson (2007). Eick et al. (1993a) analyze the SSA and the PSA for infinite-server queueing systems with periodic arrival rate and compare their results with the exact solutions.

An overview of the literature on the evaluation approaches described in this subsection is presented in Table 2.5. The approaches are applicable to a wide range of system characteristics, including abandonments and heterogeneities. However, most analyzed systems consider Poisson arrivals, and many consider exponentially distributed service times.

Table 2.5: Approaches based on piecewise stationary models (independent periods)

Reference	Queueing system				
Kolesar et al. (1975)	$M(t)$	/ $M(t)$	/ $c(t)$		
Foote (1976)	$M(t)$	/ M	/ $c(t)$		
Rider (1976)	$M(t)$	/ $M(t)$	/ 1		
Curry et al. (1978)	$M(t)$	/ M	/ c		
Newell (1979)	$M(t)$	/ D	/ 1		
Kolesar (1984)	$M(t)$	/ M	/ c	/ K	
Sze (1984)	$M(t)$	/ G	/ c		
Kwan et al. (1988)	$M(t)$	/ M	/ $c(t)$		
Agnihothri and Taylor (1991)	$M(t)$	/ PH	/ $c(t)$		
Green and Kolesar (1991)	$M(t)$	/ M	/ c		
Green et al. (1991)	$M(t)$	/ M	/ c		
Whitt (1991)	$M(t)$	/ G	/ c		
Deng et al. (1992)	$M(t)$	/ $M(t)$	/ $c(t)$		
Andrews and Parsons (1993)	$M(t)$	/ $M(t)$	/ $c(t)$		
Eick et al. (1993a)	$M(t)$	/ G	/ ∞		
Thompson (1993)	$M(t)$	/ $M(t)$	/ $c(t)$		
Green and Kolesar (1995)	$M(t)$	/ M	/ c		
Choudhury et al. (1997)	$M(t)$	/ $G(t)$	/ 1		
Green and Kolesar (1997)	$M(t)$	/ M	/ c		
Green and Kolesar (1998)	$M(t)$	/ G	/ ∞		
Kolesar and Green (1998)	$M(t)$	/ M	/ c		
Green et al. (2001)	$M(t)$	/ M	/ $c(t)$		
Ingolfsson et al. (2002)	$M(t)$	/ M	/ $c(t)$	/ K	
Green et al. (2003)	$M(t)$	/ M	/ $c(t)$		
Koole and van der Sluis (2003)	$M(t)$	/ M	/ $c(t)$		
Dietz and Vaver (2006)	$M(t)$	/ M	/ $c(t)$		
Green et al. (2006)	$M(t)$	/ M	/ $c(t)$		
De Bruin et al. (2007)	$M(t)$	/ M	/ ∞		
Ingolfsson et al. (2007)	$M(t)$	/ M	/ $c(t)$		
Steckley and Henderson (2007)	$M(t)$	/ M	/ c		$+M$
Wall and Worthington (2007)	$M(t)$	/ G	/ c		
Atlason et al. (2008)	$M(t)$	/ M	/ $c(t)$		
Liu and Wein (2008)	$M(t)$	/ M	/ c	/ K	
Singer and Donoso (2008)	$M(t)$	/ M	/ $c(t)$		
	$M(t)$	/ G	/ $c(t)$		
Stolletz (2008a)	$M(t)$	/ $M(t)$	/ $c(t)$		
Kuraya et al. (2009)	$M(t)$	/ M	/ ∞		
Manohar et al. (2009)	$M(t)$	/ $G(t)$	/ ∞		
Zhang (2009)	$M(t)$	/ M	/ c		
	$M(t)$	/ G	/ c		
Ingolfsson et al. (2010)	$M(t)$	/ M	/ $c(t)$		
Dietz (2011)	$M(t)$	/ $M(t)$	/ $c(t)$		$+M$
Stolletz (2011)	$M(t)$	/ G	/ $c(t)$		
Pang and Whitt (2012a)	$G(t)^X$	/ G^D	/ ∞		

Table 2.5: cont.

Reference	Queueing system					
Pang and Whitt (2012b)	$G(t)$	/	G^D	/	∞
Chassioti et al. (2014)	$M(t,n)$	/	G	/	c
Chen and Yang (2014)	$M(t)$	/	G	/	c
Vanberkel et al. (2014)	$M(t)$	/	G	/	∞
Selinka et al. (2016)	$M(t)$	/	M	/	c

2.3.2.2 Piecewise stationary models with linked periods

Similar to the approaches described in Section 2.3.2.1, the **stationary backlog-carryover approximation (SBC)** divides the overall time horizon into intervals and applies steady-state formulas. However, backlogs of non-served arrivals within an interval are carried over to the succeeding interval and are then considered in its performance evaluation.

Each interval is analyzed in two steps. In the first step, a loss system is assumed to calculate a backlog of unserved arrivals based on the lost jobs. These unserved arrivals are carried over to the successive interval. In the backlog calculation, the actual arrivals and the backlog of arrivals carried over from the previous interval are used as the input. In the second step, the performance measures are calculated based on the steady-state model of the corresponding waiting system. Here, a modified arrival rate is chosen such that the utilization of the waiting system equals the utilization of the loss system, as approximated in the first step.

The SBC is introduced by Stolletz (2008a) for an $M(t)/M(t)/c(t)$ system. Stolletz (2008b) extends the SBC to the analysis of $M(t)/G(t)/1$ systems. $M(t)/G/c(t)$ systems are considered by Stolletz (2011). Stolletz and Lagershausen (2013) analyze $G(t)/G/1/K$ systems. To improve the accuracy of the approximation, these authors use a variable interval length that depends on the utilization of the system. Selinka et al. (2016) extend the SBC to the analysis of a queueing system with two job classes, two server classes, and a routing decision on arrival.

To account for overload situations, the **coordinate transformation technique (CTT)** uses a model partially based on a deterministic fluid approximation (Section 2.3.3.2) that offers an accurate performance approximation for overloaded periods.

An interval's performance is calculated by using a transformation of a steady-state queueing formula. The transformation is chosen such that it converges to both the performance according to the steady-state formula for decreasing traffic intensities and the performance according to a deterministic fluid approximation for increasing traffic intensities. Such a transformation used in the analysis of an $M(t)/M(t)/1$ system is shown in Figure 2.2. As the performance at the end of an interval is used as the initial condition in the fluid approximation of the succeeding interval, the CTT integrates dependencies between successive intervals.

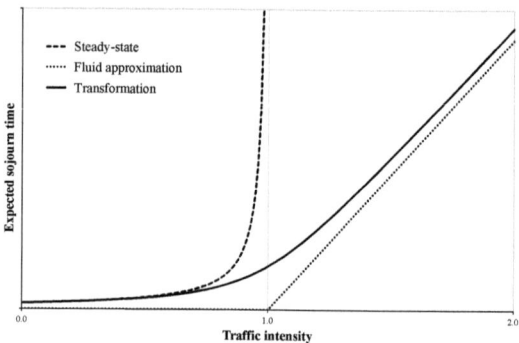

Figure 2.2: Transformation with $L^S = 0$ as initial condition (Kimber et al. (1977))

Kimber et al. (1977) introduce the CTT for an $M(t)/M(t)/1$ system. However, the shape of the time-dependent traffic intensity is restricted to a rectangular peak and adjacent-to-peak periods with a traffic intensity of zero. Kimber and Hollis (1978) extend this approach in analyzing peaks with non-zero adjacent-to-peak periods and considering general shapes of the peak traffic intensity. Catling (1977) analyzes an $M(t)/G/1$ system and allows for a general shape of the input arrival rate that is not restricted to a single peak. The CTT for $G(t)/G(t)/1$ systems with arbitrary input parameters is considered by Kimber and Daly (1986). Brilon and Wu (1990) derive a formula for the average queue length in an $M(t)/D/1$ system with a parabolic shape of the time-dependent arrival rate. Griffiths et al. (1991) expand the CTT to an $M(t)/G^{(0,s)}/1$ system with batch service up to a maximum of s jobs. However, in their version of the CTT, dependencies between successive time intervals are not considered. These dependencies are considered again by Holland and Griffiths (1999), who use the CTT to analyze the time-dependent performance of $M(t)/M^{(1,s)}/c$ systems.

Including dependencies between consecutive intervals, the SBC and the CTT take the transient behavior of a system's performance into consideration. Moreover, they can be applied to the performance evaluation of temporarily overloaded systems (Kimber and Hollis (1978), Stolletz (2008a)). The characteristics of the analyzed systems are quite different (Table 2.6). However, all but one of the cited references consider systems with an infinite waiting room.

Table 2.6: Approaches based on piecewise stationary models (linked periods)

Reference	Queueing system				
Catling (1977)	$M(t)$ /	G	/ 1		
Kimber et al. (1977)	$M(t)$ /	$M(t)$	/ 1		
Kimber and Hollis (1978)	$M(t)$ /	$M(t)$	/ 1		
Kimber and Daly (1986)	$G(t)$ /	$G(t)$	/ 1		
Brilon and Wu (1990)	$M(t)$ /	D	/ 1		
Griffiths et al. (1991)	$M(t)$ /	$G^{(0,s)}$	/ 1		
Holland and Griffiths (1999)	$M(t)$ /	$M^{(1,s)}$	/ c		
Stolletz (2008a)	$M(t)$ /	$M(t)$	/ $c(t)$		
Stolletz (2008b)	$M(t)$ /	$G(t)$	/ 1		
Stolletz (2011)	$M(t)$ /	G	/ $c(t)$		
Chen et al. (2013)	$M(t)$ /	E_k	/ $c(t)$		
Stolletz and Lagershausen (2013)	$G(t)$ /	G	/ 1	/ K	
Selinka et al. (2016)	$M(t)$ /	M	/ c		

2.3.2.3 Piecewise transient models

The approaches described in this paragraph are **based on transient models (BOT)** that are used to analyze consecutive intervals with constant input parameters. The system state at the end of an interval serves as initial condition for the performance evaluation of the subsequent interval.

The transient solution of a queueing system with a finite waiting room is used by Upton and Tripathi (1982) to approximate the performance of an $M(t)/M/1$ system with an infinite waiting room. Choudhury et al. (1997) use numerical transform inversion and apply transient models to analyze an $M(t)/G(t)/1$ system. Parthasarathy and Sudhesh (2006) derive the exact transient solution for an $M/M/1$ system by using generating functions and then apply it to an $M(t)/M(t)/1$ system with piecewise constant input parameters. This approach is extended by Griffiths et al. (2008) to the case of Erlang-distributed service times. Duda (1986), Czachórski et al. (2009), and Czachórski et al. (2010) use the diffusion approximation for the transient performance evaluation (see also Section 2.3.3.2).

A common approximation technique for the transient analysis of Markovian queueing systems is the **uniformization/randomization (UR)** approximation. This approach analyzes the transient performance of a continuous-time Markov chain (CTMC) by transformation in a discrete-time Markov chain (DTMC).

The transition probability matrix $\mathbf{A}$ of the DTMC is derived by the uniformization of the generator matrix of the original CTMC. If the overall outgoing transition rates are identical for all states in the CTMC, the probability $g(j)$ for j transitions within one evaluation interval of the DTMC follows a Poisson distribution. Thus, self-transitions are included to unify the overall transition rates out of every state in the original CTMC. Then, the state probability vector $\mathbf{P}(i)$ at the end of interval i can be calculated according to Equation (2.6), where $\mathbf{A}^j$ denotes a j-times multiplication of the matrix $\mathbf{A}$ by itself. Here, the transitions within an interval are randomized according to the Poisson distribution mentioned above. Only a maximum of m possible transitions within one interval is considered to preserve computational tractability. The chosen value of m must be sufficiently large to achieve a reasonable approximation quality of the infinite number of possible state transitions

$$\mathbf{P}(i) = \sum_{j=0}^{m} g(j) \cdot \mathbf{P}(i-1) \cdot \mathbf{A}^j. \tag{2.6}$$

To account for non-stationary input parameters, the time-dependent generator matrix and the resulting time-dependent transition probability matrix must be considered.

Grassmann (1977a) reports the first study to use the concept of the uniformization/randomization approximation. Here, the transient behavior of an $M/M/1$ system is analyzed, but only constant input parameters are considered. However, the applicability of the approach to the analysis of time-dependent systems is mentioned by Gross and Miller (1984) and assessed for general Markovian systems by Van Dijk (1992). Dormuth and Alfa (1997) apply the uniformization/randomization approach in the performance analysis of an $MAP(t)/PH(t)/1/K$ system. Furthermore, they extend the approach by incorporating an online adaptation of the length of the discretization intervals to improve the performance approximation. Flexible interval lengths are also included in the modification of Arns et al. (2010). Although their approach is applicable to general Markovian systems, it is applied to the analysis of an $M(t)/M(t)/1/K$ system in their numerical study. Creemers et al. (2014) apply the uniformization/randomization approximation in the analysis of $PH(t)/PH(t)/c(t) + PH(t)$ systems with limited and unlimited waiting rooms to approximate queueing systems with general distributions.

A major advantage of the uniformization/randomization approach is its applicability to any Markovian queueing system. Furthermore, the complete time-dependent distribution of the state probabilities is derived

(Gross and Miller (1984)). However, the approach is characterized by high computation times (Grassmann (1977b), Ingolfsson et al. (2007)). Table 2.7 shows that piecewise transient models can be used in the performance evaluation of a wide range of system configurations. Such models require only a tractable method for the transient analysis with arbitrary initial conditions.

Table 2.7: Approaches based on piecewise transient models

Reference	Queueing system				
Upton and Tripathi (1982)	$M(t)$	/ M	/ 1		
Gross and Miller (1984)	$M(t)$	/ $M(t)$	/ $c(t)$	/ K	
Mok and Shanthikumar (1987)	$M(t)$	/ M	/ $c(t)$	/ K	$+M$
Choudhury et al. (1997)	$M(t)$	/ $G(t)$	/ 1		
Dormuth and Alfa (1997)	$MAP(t)$	/ $PH(t)$	/ 1	/ K	
Hebert and Dietz (1997)	$M(t)$	/ $PH(t)$	/ 1		
Parthasarathy and Sudhesh (2006)	$M(t)$	/ $M(t)$	/ 1		
Ingolfsson et al. (2007)	$M(t)$	/ M	/ $c(t)$		
Griffiths et al. (2008)	$M(t)$	/ E_k	/ 1		
Arns et al. (2010)	$M(t)$	/ $M(t)$	/ 1	/ K	
Ingolfsson et al. (2010)	$M(t)$	/ M	/ $c(t)$		
Creemers et al. (2014)	$G(t)$	/ $G(t)$	/ $c(t)$		$+G(t)$
	$G(t)$	/ $G(t)$	/ $c(t)$	/ K	$+G(t)$

The underlying idea of the **discrete-time approach (DTA)** is to replace the continuous time with discrete points in time at which the system state is observed. The use of this approach leads to an approximation error if the system does not operate with time slots. The state probabilities for the next observation point are obtained by multiplying the state probability vector of the current observation point with a time-dependent transition probability matrix. The evolution of the system performance over time is then obtained through recursive vector matrix multiplications. In contrast to the UR, which discretizes a CTMC via uniformization, the DTA directly assumes that time is discrete and that only one transition per interval is possible. Depending on the queueing system and the length of the discretization interval, one transition accounts for multiple arrivals and/or multiple service completions.

Galliher and Wheeler (1958) introduce the basic idea for an $M(t)/D(t)/c(t)$ system. Setting the interval length equal to the service time is reported to work well if the deterministic service time is rather short compared with the time interval of interest. Otherwise, Minh (1978) suggests modifying the interval length and introducing auxiliary state variables for the remaining service time in addition to the number of jobs in the system. This concept is also used by Alfa (1982), Omosigho and Worthington (1985), Omosigho and Worthington (1988), Brahimi and Worthington (1991a), Brahimi and Worthington (1991b), Mejía-Téllez and Worthington (1994), and Chassioti and Worthington (2004) to model a general service time distribution. Regarding the arrival process, these models require only that the number of arrivals in each discretization interval be an independent random variable. This assumption allows for time-dependent Poisson processes, potentially with batch arrivals, and $D^{X(t)}$ arrival processes where the inter-arrival time is equal to the interval length and where the batch size distribution X is time-dependent. Although Powell and Simão (1986) call their approach numerical simulation, they use the same technique of auxiliary variables in analyzing a discrete-time $M(t)^X/G(t)^Y/1/K$ bulk queue with a random number of Y jobs that can be served simultaneously under different dispatching rules for the server. Kahraman and Gosavi (2011) focus on stranded customers, i.e., unserved customers that remain in the queue directly after the visit of the server, and consider different dispatching rules. Alfa (1990) and Alfa and Chen (1991) avoid the use of computationally expensive auxiliary variables by approximating the probability of an empty system by using the Maximum Entropy Principle. The expected queue length is then obtained based on the probability of an empty system. Using an approach unlike the approaches discussed so far, Moore (1975) observes the system state at the departure time of the jobs from the queue. At these observation points, the expected queue length of an $M(t)^{X(t)}/E_k/1$ system is computed. Worthington and Wall (1999) provide a survey of most of the existing DTAs for systems with time-dependent Markovian arrival processes, generally distributed service times, and single or multiple servers.

Table 2.8: Discrete-time approaches

Reference	Queueing system			
Galliher and Wheeler (1958)	$M(t)$	/ $D(t)$	/ $c(t)$	
Koopman (1972)	$M(t)$	/ D	/ 1	/ K
Moore (1975)	$M(t)^{X(t)}$	/ E_k	/ 1	
Minh (1978)	$M(t)^X$	/ G	/ 1	
Alfa (1982)	$M(t)^X$	/ G^Y	/ 1	
	$M(t)^X$	/ G^Y	/ 1	/ K
Upton and Tripathi (1982)	$M(t)$	/ M	/ 1	
Omosigho and Worthington (1985)	$M(t)^{X(t)}$	/ G	/ 1	/ K
	$D^{X(t)}$	/ G	/ 1	/ K
Powell and Simão (1986)	$M(t)^X$	/ $G(t)^Y$	/ 1	/ K
	$D^{X(t)}$	/ $G(t)^Y$	/ 1	/ K
Omosigho and Worthington (1988)	$M(t)^{X(t)}$	/ G	/ 1	/ K
	$D^{X(t)}$	/ G	/ 1	/ K
Alfa (1990)	$M(t)$	/ D	/ 1	
Brilon and Wu (1990)	$M(t)$	/ D	/ 1	
	$D^{X(t)}$	/ D	/ 1	
Alfa and Chen (1991)	$M(t)$	/ G	/ 1	
Brahimi and Worthington (1991a)	$D^{X(t)}$	/ G	/ 1	
Brahimi and Worthington (1991b)	$M(t)$	/ G	/ c	/ K
	$D^{X(t)}$	/ G	/ c	/ K
Lackman et al. (1992)	$M(t)$	/ D	/ $1+D$	
	$M(t)$	/ D	/ $1+D$	/ NPPrio
Mejía-Téllez and Worthington (1994)	$M(t)$	/ $G^{(0,s)}$	/ 1	
Daniel (1995)	$M(t)$	/ D	/ c	/ K
Bennett and Worthington (1998)	$D^{X(t)}$	/ G	/ 1	
Daniel and Pahwa (2000)	$M(t)$	/ D	/ c	/ K
Chassioti and Worthington (2004)	$M(t)$	/ G	/ $c(t)$	
	$M(t)$	/ G	/ $c(t)$	/ K
Wall and Worthington (2007)	$M(t)$	/ G	/ c	
	$D^{X(t)}$	/ G	/ c	
Alfa and Margolius (2008)	$M(t)$	/ $M(t)$	/ $c(t)$	
Daniel and Harback (2008)	$M(t)$	/ D	/ c	/ K
Daniel and Harback (2009)	$M(t)$	/ D	/ c	/ K
Viti and van Zuylen (2009)	$M(t)$	/ $D(t)$	/ 1	/ K
Viti and van Zuylen (2010)	$M(t)$	/ $D(t)$	/ 1	/ K
Kahraman and Gosavi (2011)	$M(t)$	/ G^Y	/ 1	
Blumberg-Nitzani and Bar-Gera (2014)	$D^{X(t)}$	/ D	/ 1	

The main advantage of the DTA is its flexibility with respect to the service time distribution (see Table 2.8) and the derivation of the time-dependent probability distribution for the complete state space. Hence, the approach allows one to obtain quantiles of the number of jobs in the system and the distribution of the virtual waiting time (Minh (1978), Wall and Worthington (2007)). The major disadvantage of the DTA is the rapidly growing state space with an increasing waiting room and the need for an additional auxiliary variable for every additional server.

2.3.3 Approaches based on modified system characteristics

2.3.3.1 Modified number of servers

Although most real systems have a finite number of servers, the explicit results for infinite-server systems gain relevance in approximation approaches. An overview of the literature on these approaches is presented in Table 2.9.

In queueing systems with an infinite number of parallel servers, the time-dependent number of busy servers $L^B(t)$ is comparatively easy to determine (see Section 2.3.1). Thus, this number can be used to estimate performance measures of systems with a finite number of servers. Such an **infinite-server approximation (INFSA)** is applied by Jennings et al. (1996) to analyze the probability of waiting in a $G(t)/G(t)/c(t)$ system. They use a normal approximation to estimate the distribution of busy servers in the infinite-server system and apply their results to derive a staffing formula. Feldman et al. (2008) use such an INFSA to analyze $M(t)/G/c(t) + G$ systems. Liu and Whitt (2012a) derive a *delayed-infinite-server (DIS)* approximation model that is applied in a staffing algorithm for an $M(t)/G/c(t) + G$ system by decomposing the original system into two infinite-server systems – one representing the waiting jobs including abandonments and the other representing the jobs in service.

The key idea of the **modified offered load approach (MOL)** is the approximation of the time-dependent offered load in a queueing system by the number of busy servers in the corresponding system with an infinite number of servers. Based on this relation, a modified arrival rate is derived, and this arrival rate is then used to calculate the system's performance for every point in time by using steady-state models. In doing so, the MOL takes advantage of the known solution of the DE describing the number of jobs in an infinite-server system (see Section 2.3.1).

For an $M(t)/M(t)/\infty$ queueing system, the expected number $L^S(t) = L^B(t)$ of busy servers at time t is given by Equation (2.5). The modified arrival rate $\lambda^{MAR}(t) = \mathrm{E}[L^B(t)] \cdot \mu(t)$ is chosen such that the expected number of busy servers in the stationary $M/M/c$ system equals the expected number of busy servers in the time-dependent infinite-server system.

Jagerman (1975) introduces the MOL to analyze the blocking probability in $M(t)/M/c/c$ systems. The applicability of the MOL to the analysis of more general queueing systems with waiting rooms is mentioned by Jennings et al. (1996). Massey and Whitt (1997) apply the MOL to evaluate an $M(t)/M/c$ system and compare their results with the numerical solution of the CKEs. Feldman et al. (2008) extend the MOL to analyze $M(t)/G/c(t) + G$ systems. In addition to the DIS approach mentioned above, Liu and Whitt (2012a) develop the DIS-MOL, which is an extension in which the offered load in the queue, representing the jobs in service, is used as an input for a stationary $M/G/c + G$ system. Using an approach similar to the MOL, Yom-Tov and Mandelbaum (2014) use the time-dependent number of busy servers in an infinite-server system as the input in their staffing algorithm for an $M(t)/G/c(t)$ system.

In contrast to the methods described in Section 2.3.2.1, the MOL does not analyze the performance of intervals independently. Nevertheless, as the derivation of the modified arrival rate corresponds to the calculation of the exponentially weighted moving average over the period $[-\infty, t]$, the MOL is similar to the EAA and the RA described in Section 2.3.2.1, which also use a moving average as the input in the performance calculations according to steady-state formulas (Ingolfsson et al. (2007)). The transient behavior and dependencies between intervals are taken into account in the derivation of the modified arrival rate. Thus, the MOL has a structure similar to the SBC (Section 2.3.2.2). Owing to the application of infinite-server systems, the approximation quality of the MOL renders this approach more suitable for systems with a decreasing probability of waiting, i.e., an increasing number of servers or decreasing traffic intensity (Jennings and Massey (1997), Massey and Whitt (1997)). Additionally, the approximation quality decreases with increasing rate of change in the input arrival rate (Jagerman (1975)). Jennings and Massey (1997) show that the idea of the MOL is applicable to any time-dependent system if its state space is a subset of the state space of a larger system for which the performance is simpler to evaluate. Massey (2002) provides an overview through 2002 of the literature on approaches that use the explicit solution of infinite-server systems.

Table 2.9: Infinite-server approximations

Reference	Queueing system						
Sze (1984)	$M(t)$ / G / c						
Jennings et al. (1996)	$G(t)$ / $G(t)$ / $c(t)$						
Green and Kolesar (1997)	$M(t)$ / M / c						
Massey and Whitt (1997)	$M(t)$ / M / c						
Ingolfsson et al. (2007)	$M(t)$ / M / $c(t)$						
Feldman et al. (2008)	$M(t)$ / G / $c(t)$	$+G$					
Liu and Wein (2008)	$M(t)$ / M / c / K / PPrio						
Liu and Whitt (2012a)	$M(t)$ / G / $c(t)$	$+G$					
Yom-Tov and Mandelbaum (2014)	$M(t)$ / G / $c(t)$						

2.3.3.2 Modified job characteristics

The fluid approximation, the pointwise stationary fluid flow approximation, and the diffusion approximation replace discrete jobs with a continuum. These approaches differ in the way that they consider stochasticity. The fourth approach, the uniform acceleration, modifies the arrival and service rate of the jobs.

The key idea of the **fluid approximation (FLUID)** is to replace randomly arriving discrete jobs with a deterministic continuum. This continuum can be interpreted as a fluid that flows with rate $\lambda(t)$ into a reservoir. The service process is approximated by a deterministic outflow from the reservoir. The level of fluid in the reservoir then serves as an approximation for the number of jobs in the system. The derivative with respect to time of the fluid level for a queueing system with c parallel servers without a queue length limit is given by

$$
\mathrm{E}[L^S(t)]' = \begin{cases} 0, & \text{if } \mathrm{E}[L^S(t)] = 0 \wedge \lambda(t) \leq \mu(t) \cdot c \\ \lambda(t) - \mu(t) \cdot \min\{c; \mathrm{E}[L^S(t)]\}, & \text{otherwise.} \end{cases} \tag{2.7}
$$

The fluid approximation represents one of the first approaches for the analysis of time-dependent queueing systems. It is described in the book of Newell (1971) as engineering approach for the performance evaluation of systems for which temporary overload rather than randomness is the primary reason for the existence of queues. A direct application of the fluid approximation can be found in Horonjeff (1969), Koopman (1972), Wirasinghe and Shehata (1988), and Janic (2009). It is also used by Harrison and Zeevi (2005) and Swaroop et al. (2012) within optimization approaches. Mandelbaum et al. (2002) investigate a fluid approximation for an $M(t)/M(t)/c(t) + M(t)$ system with retrials. An adjusted fluid approximation for this system is proposed by Ko and Gautam (2013). Aguir et al. (2004) modify the queueing model and include the effect of balking but assume a time-invariant service rate. By choosing a balking probability of 0 if $L^S < K$ and 1 otherwise, their model can also approximate systems with a finite waiting room. Whitt (1999) develops the fluid approximation for an $M(t)/G/c/$PPrio system by reducing the service rate of a given class by the demand of all higher classes. Ridley et al. (2004) derive the fluid approximation for a two-class $M(t)/M/c/$PPrio system that is supported by a limit theorem. Ko and Gautam (2010) propose a

Gaussian-based adjustment of the fluid approximation for a system with servers that switch between an active and an inactive pool.

Hampshire et al. (2009) combine the fluid approximation with the MOL approach (see Section 2.3.3.1) to analyze the abandonments and blocking probability in an $M(t)/M/c(t)/K(t) + M$ system. Liu and Whitt (2012b) introduce the fluid approximation for a $G(t)/G/c(t) + G$ system. They separately track the fluid in the queue and on the servers. For both parts, two-parameter functions $L^Q(t, y)$ and $L^S(t, y)$ describe the amount of fluid at time t that has spent at most y time units in the queue and on the server, respectively. Thus, abandonments can be treated as a proportion of the fluid that leaves the queue without being served depending on y. The authors develop an algorithm that generates approximations for $E[L^Q(t)]$ and $E[L^S(t)]$, as well as for the expected head of line and virtual waiting time. Liu and Whitt (2011) use this modeling approach to establish an asymptotic loss of memory property for a $G(t)/M(t)/c(t) + G(t)$ fluid approximation, i.e., the performance of the queue becomes asymptotically independent of the initial condition as time proceeds.

Apart from the use of the fluid approximation for performance evaluation, another literature stream establishes fluid limits for stochastic queueing systems. The existence of such fluid limits supports the use of the fluid approximation, particularly under heavy traffic. For a more in-depth discussion on fluid limits and their derivation, see Jiménez and Koole (2004), Liu and Whitt (2014), and the references therein. As Table 2.10 shows, the fluid approximation is often used for queueing systems with stochastic inter-arrival and service times. However, for periods of persistent underload, the fluid approximation predicts an empty system since it neglects randomness as a reason for the occurrence of queues. Pender (2014b) notes that a deterministic surrogate distribution also leads to a fluid approximation. The fluid approximation gains additional relevance as integral part of other analytical approaches, namely, in the CTT (Section 2.3.2.2) and in the pointwise stationary fluid flow approximation, which is described in the next paragraph.

The **pointwise stationary fluid flow approximation (PSFFA)** combines the deterministic fluid approximation with steady-state queueing formulas to integrate stochasticity. The fluid flow described by Equation (2.7) is modified such that the outflow from the system depends on the server utilization. The utilization is approximated by the inverse of stationary queueing formulas such that the utilization becomes a function of the expected number of jobs in the system $E[U(t)] = g^{-1}(E[L^S(t)], c)$. All parameters are assumed to be constant, and the queueing system is assumed to be in the steady state at time t, i.e., pointwise stationary (Section 2.3.2.1). The resulting DE (2.8) can be integrated numerically to obtain the expected number of jobs in the system over time

$$E[L^S(t)]' = \lambda(t) - \mu(t) \cdot c \cdot g^{-1}(E[L^S(t)], c). \tag{2.8}$$

A finite waiting room causes blocking and reduces the effective arrival rate. Consequently, for finite waiting rooms, an additional function that relates the blocking probability to the expected number of jobs in the system is required. Chen et al. (2011) note that Equation (2.8) can be used directly for queueing systems with a finite waiting room by solving it subject to the constraint $E[L^S(t)] \leq K$.

Agnew (1976) reports the first attempt to relate the outflow of a fluid queue to the expected number of jobs in the system. He derives general properties of the function $E[U] = g^{-1}(E[L^S(t)], 1)$ and notes that this function can be either determined through statistical analysis from real systems or determined analytically. Tipper and Sundareshan (1990) analyze a heterogeneous $M(t)/M/1$ system where arrivals originate from multiple independent sources. They introduce a DE similar to Equation (2.8) for the total number of jobs in the system and one additional equation for each job class. Coining term PSFFA, Wang et al. (1996) provide approximations for $M(t)/G/1$, $G(t)/G/1$, and $M(t)/M/1/K$ systems. Chen et al. (2013) invert the approximation of Cosmetatos (1976) numerically with a bisection method and, thus, extend the approach to a multi-server

$M(t)/E_k/c(t)$ system. Based on a data set, Xu et al. (2014) use polynomial curve fitting to derive $g^{-1}(\mathrm{E}[L^S(t)], 1)$.

The PSFFA delivers results only for the expected value of the number of jobs in the system. Higher moments remain intractable. $\mathrm{E}[L^S(t)]$ converges to exact steady-state values for constant parameters if the inverse function $g^{-1}(\mathrm{E}[L^S(t)], c)$ is exact. However, Tipper and Sundareshan (1990) and Wang et al. (1996) report that the PSFFA reaches the steady state too rapidly. This leads to an overestimation of peaks and an underestimation of valleys for quickly varying input rates. Although the PSFFA and the SDA (Section 2.3.1) are independently developed approaches, they share the same MDE as the starting point, i.e., for $c = 1$, Equation (2.2) simplifies to Equation (2.8) (Filipiak (1984)). The approaches differ in how they obtain the unknown probability $1 - P_0 = \mathrm{E}[U]$.

The **diffusion approximation (DIFF)** replaces the mathematically intractable discrete stochastic process $L^S(t)$ with a continuous stochastic process $\mathcal{X}(t)$ which is known as Brownian motion. The incremental changes $d\mathcal{X}(t) = \mathcal{X}(t + dt) - \mathcal{X}(t)$ are normally distributed with infinitesimal mean $b dt$ and infinitesimal variance $a dt$. For a non-empty system, the stochastic process $\mathcal{X}(t)$ is described by diffusion equation (2.9)

$$\frac{\partial f(x, t)}{\partial t} = \frac{a(t)}{2} \cdot \frac{\partial^2 f(x, t)}{\partial x^2} - b(t) \cdot \frac{\partial f(x, t)}{\partial x}. \tag{2.9}$$

Equation (2.9) is also known as the Kolmogorov or Fokker-Planck equation with probability density function $f(x, t)$ and x as a continuous approximation of the number of jobs in the system. Depending on $a(t)$ and $b(t)$ as well as on the boundary conditions, explicit solutions of the partial differential equation (2.9) exist; otherwise, it must be solved numerically. The diffusion approximation goes along with three key modeling decisions. (i) Depending on the system characteristics, $a(t)$ and $b(t)$ must be chosen. They either are a function of time (Newell (1968a)) or are assumed to be piecewise constant, and transient solutions are combined as described in Section 2.3.2.3 (Duda (1986)). (ii) Boundary conditions must be imposed to model the behavior of the stochastic process if the system is empty or, if applicable, if it reaches its waiting room limit K. For heavy traffic situations, Equation (2.9) is typically solved subject to boundary conditions. This leads to a reflected Brownian motion, i.e., trajectories of $\mathcal{X}(t)$ do not spend time at the boundary but are directly reflected. Such a condition does not work for underload situations, as idle times of the server must be taken into account. Thus, elementary return barriers are imposed, which ensure that $\mathcal{X}(t)$ stays in a boundary state for a certain period of time according to a stochastic holding time distribution. (iii) Only the moments of $L^S(t)$ may be directly approximated by their equivalents of $\mathcal{X}(t)$. To obtain the state probabilities $P_n(t)$, the continuous density function $f(x, t)$ must be re-discretized (Duda (1986)).

In his pioneering works, Newell (1968a,b,c) proposes the diffusion approximation for $G(t)/G/1$ systems. He considers the case of a rush hour caused by an increasing arrival rate that eventually exceeds the service rate and then returns to values below the service rate. Knessl (2000) provides an exact solution of the diffusion process for $\rho \approx 1$ with an initially empty queue, which is generalized to arbitrary initial conditions by Knessl and Yang (2001). Both models assume that $\rho(t)$ either is linear in t or increases in a single step. Giorno et al. (1987) propose the diffusion approximation for the queue length distribution of the $M(t, n)/M(t, n)/1$ system. In their study, the arrival and service rates are time- and state-dependent such that they increase with the number of jobs n in the system. Their findings resemble the results of the special case discussed by Clarke (1956). Di Crescenzo and Nobile (1995) also analyze an $M(t, n)/M(t, n)/1$ system but use a more general arrival rate function that includes the model by Giorno et al. (1987) as a special case. Ko and Gautam (2010) obtain an adjusted diffusion model by using an adjusted fluid approximation. Mandelbaum et al. (2002) provide numerical results for the diffusion approximation of an $M(t)/M(t)/c(t) + M(t)$ system with retrials, which is based on a limit theorem established by Mandelbaum et al. (1998). The adjusted version of the limit theorem by Ko and Gautam (2013) improves the approximation quality of the diffusion approximation for systems with a small number of servers and for $E[L^S(t)]$ close to $c(t)$. Massey and Pender (2013) show that their SDA is equivalent to the approach of Ko and Gautam (2013). Filipiak (1983) suggests moving the reflecting barrier from 0 to -1 to approximate underload situations in an $M(t)/M(t)/1$ system. Following the idea of a piecewise transient analysis (Section 2.3.2.3), Duda (1986) proposes an elementary return barrier diffusion approximation with Coxian distributed holding times at the return barrier for the transient solution of a $G/G/1$ system. Czachórski et al. (2009) and Czachórski et al. (2010) introduce another elementary return barrier with exponentially distributed holding times to model a finite waiting room for a $G/G/1/K/$PPrio system with multiple job classes and a simple $G/G/1/K$ system, respectively. Kimura (2004) provides a limited survey with respect to time-dependent and steady-state diffusion models.

The diffusion approximation can be used for non-Markovian systems since $a(t)$ and $b(t)$ depend on the means and variances of the arrival and service processes (Table 2.10). In addition, the use of the diffusion approximation for such systems results in an approximation of the complete probability distribution of $L^S(t)$. Further, it is rigorously supported by limit theorems and results of the uniform acceleration technique, which is described in detail in the next paragraph.

The **uniform acceleration (UA)** technique simultaneously increases the arrival and service rate such that their ratio remains fixed. UA may be regarded as the non-stationary analogue to steady-state analysis (Massey (2002)). Similar to the INFSA, which utilizes the tractability of infinite-server systems, the derived scaled queueing systems allow for an enhanced analytical understanding of the time-dependent behavior.

Keller (1982) reports the first attempt to use this scaling. Starting with the discrete stochastic process, he provides an attempt to rigorously derive

Newell's diffusion approximation. Massey (1985) coins the term UA and proposes

$$\rho^*(t_0, t) = \sup_{0 \le t_0 \le t} \frac{\int_{t_0}^{t} \lambda(\tau)\,d\tau}{\int_{t_0}^{t} \mu(\tau)\,d\tau} \tag{2.10}$$

as a modified parameter to differentiate between underloaded and overloaded queues. The results are refined by Yin and Zhang (2002). Mandelbaum and Massey (1995) apply UA to the sample path of an $M(t)/M(t)/1$ system and obtain an asymptotic expansion. Yang and Knessl (1997) correct the results of Keller (1982) and further extend them to general service processes. Flick and Liao (2010) extend the approach of Massey (1985) to queueing systems with more than one server. The case of finite waiting rooms is treated by Tan et al. (2013).

The results of the UA serve as rigorous justification for the PSA, the fluid approximation, and the diffusion approximation. These results suggest that the PSA works well for underloaded queues (Flick and Liao (2010)) and that overloaded queues are well approximated by the fluid approximation (Mandelbaum and Massey (1995)). In addition, these findings substantiate the core idea of the CTT.

Table 2.10: Approximations based on modified job characteristics

Reference	Queueing system				
Fluid approximation					
Newell (1968b)	$G(t)$	/ G	/ 1		
Gaver (1969)	$D(t)$	/ $D(t)$	/ 1		
Horonjeff (1969)	$D(t)$	/ $D(t)$	/ 1		
Paullin and Horonjeff (1969)	$D(t)$	/ D	/ c		
Newell (1971)	$D(t)$	/ $D(t)$	/ 1		
Koopman (1972)	$D(t)$	/ D	/ 1	/ K	
Newell (1979)	$D(t)$	/ D	/ 1		
de Neufville and Grillot (1982)	$D(t)$	/ D	/ 1		
Wirasinghe and Shehata (1988)	$D(t)$	/ D	/ 1		
Jung and Lee (1989a)	$G(t)$	/ G	/ $c(t)$		
Wirasinghe and Bandara (1990)	$D(t)$	/ D	/ c		
Whitt (1999)	$M(t)$	/ G	/ c		/ PPrio
Mandelbaum et al. (2002)	$M(t)$	/ $M(t)$	/ $c(t)$		$+M(t)$

Reference	Queueing system							
Aguir et al. (2004)	$M(t)$	/	M	/	$c(t)$			$+M$
	$M(t)$	/	M	/	$c(t)$	/	K	$+M$
Jiménez and Koole (2004)	$M(t)$	/	M	/	c			
Ridley et al. (2004)	$M(t)$	/	M	/	c			/ PPrio
De Barros and Tomber (2007)	$D(t)$	/	D	/	1			
Kuwahara (2007)	$D(t)$	/	D	/	1			
Hampshire et al. (2009)	$M(t)$	/	M	/	$c(t)$	/	$K(t)$	$+M$
Janic (2009)	$D(t)$	/	$D(t)$	/	1			
Viti and van Zuylen (2009)	$M(t)$	/	$D(t)$	/	1	/	K	
Bertsimas and Doan (2010)	$M(t)$	/	M	/	$c(t)$			$+M$
Chen and Yang (2010)	$D(t)$	/	D	/	1			
Ko and Gautam (2010)	$M(t)$	/	M	/	$c(t)$			
Viti and van Zuylen (2010)	$M(t)$	/	$D(t)$	/	1	/	K	
Liu and Whitt (2011)	$G(t)$	/	$M(t)$	/	$c(t)$			$+G(t)$
Stolletz (2011)	$M(t)$	/	G	/	$c(t)$			
Liu and Whitt (2012b)	$G(t)$	/	G	/	$c(t)$			$+G$
Swaroop et al. (2012)	$D(t)$	/	D	/	1			
Ko and Gautam (2013)	$M(t)$	/	$M(t)$	/	$c(t)$			$+M(t)$
Massey and Pender (2013)	$M(t)$	/	M	/	$c(t)$			$+M$
Chen and Yang (2014)	$M(t)$	/	G	/	c			
Pender (2014a)	$M(t)$	/	$M(t)$	/	$c(t)$			$+M(t)$

Pointwise stationary fluid flow approximation

Agnew (1976)	$G(t)$	/	G	/	1			
Filipiak (1984)	$M(t)$	/	M	/	1			
Tipper and Sundareshan (1990)	$M(t)$	/	M	/	1			
Wang et al. (1996)	$M(t)$	/	G	/	1			
	$G(t)$	/	G	/	1			
	$M(t)$	/	M	/	1	/	K	
Chen et al. (2011)	$M(t)$	/	G	/	1			
Chen et al. (2013)	$M(t)$	/	E_k	/	$c(t)$			
Chen et al. (2013)	$M(t)$	/	E_k	/	$c(t)$			
Chen et al. (2013)	$M(t)$	/	E_k	/	$c(t)$			
Yang et al. (2013)	$M(t)$	/	E_k	/	$c(t)$			
Chen and Yang (2014)	$M(t)$	/	G	/	c			
Xu et al. (2014)	$D(t)$	/	D	/	1			

Diffusion approximation

Newell (1968a)	$G(t)$	/	G	/	1			
Newell (1968b)	$G(t)$	/	G	/	1			
Newell (1968c)	$G(t)$	/	G	/	1			
Keller (1982)	$M(t)$	/	$M(t)$	/	1			
Filipiak (1983)	$M(t)$	/	$M(t)$	/	1			
Duda (1986)	$G(t)$	/	$G(t)$	/	1			
Giorno et al. (1987)	$M(t,n)$	/	$M(t,n)$	/	1			
Jung and Lee (1989a)	$G(t)$	/	G	/	$c(t)$	/	K	
Di Crescenzo and Nobile (1995)	$M(t,n)$	/	$M(t,n)$	/	1			
Knessl (2000)	$G(t)$	/	$G(t)$	/	1			
Knessl and Yang (2001)	$G(t)$	/	$G(t)$	/	1			
Mandelbaum et al. (2002)	$M(t)$	/	$M(t)$	/	$c(t)$			$+M(t)$
Janic (2005)	$G(t)$	/	$G(t)$	/	1			

Table 2.10: cont.

Reference	Queueing system								
Czachórski et al. (2009)	$G(t)$	/	G	/	1	/	K	/	PPrio
Czachórski et al. (2010)	$G(t)$	/	G	/	1	/	K		
Ko and Gautam (2010)	$M(t)$	/	M	/	$c(t)$				
Ko and Gautam (2013)	$M(t)$	/	$M(t)$	/	$c(t)$	+	$M(t)$		
Lovell et al. (2013)	$G(t)$	/	$G(t)$	/	1	/	K		
Massey and Pender (2013)	$M(t)$	/	M	/	$c(t)$	+	M		
Pender (2014a)	$M(t)$	/	$M(t)$	/	$c(t)$	+	$M(t)$		
Uniform acceleration									
Keller (1982)	$M(t)$	/	$M(t)$	/	1				
Massey (1985)	$M(t)$	/	$M(t)$	/	1				
Mandelbaum and Massey (1995)	$M(t)$	/	$M(t)$	/	1				
Yang and Knessl (1997)	$M(t)$	/	G	/	1				
Yin and Zhang (2002)	$M(t)$	/	$M(t)$	/	1				
Flick and Liao (2010)	$M(t)$	/	$M(t)$	/	c				
Tan et al. (2013)	$M(t)$	/	M	/	1	/	K		

2.4 Methodological relations and numerical comparisons

The classification scheme introduced in Section 2.2 groups approaches that share a common idea in their analysis. In addition, we discuss links between approaches in Section 2.3. These links are summarized in Figure 2.3, which reveals that there are links between approaches not only within classification categories but also beyond category boundaries.

Besides the identified methodological links, some approaches are compared numerically in the literature. References that include numerical studies comparing two or more approaches for single-, multi-, and infinite-server systems are listed in Table 2.11. The majority of these numerical studies focus on multi-server systems with Markovian properties. Further, some studies include general distributions, abandonments, or heterogeneities. From a methodological point of view, it becomes apparent that a popular benchmark is the numerical solution of the CKEs, as the approximation error then originates only from the numerical solution scheme. Ingolfsson et al. (2007) compare approaches from all three main cate-

	Numerical and analytical solutions				Approaches based on models with piecewise constant parameters								Approaches based on modified system characteristics					
	CKE	SDA	SASN	EXPL	SSA	SIPP	PSA	SBC	CTT	BOT	UR	DTA	INFSA	MOL	FLUID	PSFFA	DIFF	UA
CKE		X	X	X														
SDA	X													X	X			
SASN	X																	
EXPL	X												X	X				
SSA					X	X												
SIPP					X		X	X	X									
PSA					X	X									X			X
SBC							X		X				X					
CTT							X	X							X			X
BOT																X		
UR												X						
DTA										X								
INFSA			X										X					
MOL			X					X					X					
FLUID	X							X							X			X
PSFFA	X						X								X			
DIFF										X								X
UA							X	X							X	X		

Figure 2.3: Methodological links between approaches for the performance evaluation of time-dependent systems

gories of our classification scheme for an $M(t)/M/c(t)$ system. Apart from that study, most studies compare approaches within a single category. The quality of approximation approaches strongly depends on the system parameters. Nevertheless, some conclusions with respect to the applicability of a subset of the discussed approaches are provided by Stolletz (2008b) and Chen et al. (2013).

Table 2.11: Numerical comparisons of time-dependent queueing systems

Reference	Compared methods	Queueing system	Performance measures
Single-server queueing systems ($c = 1$)			
Leese and Boyd (1966)	CKE, SASN	$M(t)/M/1$	$L^Q(t)$
Newell (1968b)	DIFF, FLUID	$G(t)/G/1$	$E[L^S(t)]$
Koopman (1972)	CKE, DTA, FLUID	$M(t)/G(t)/1/K$	$E[L^Q(t)]$
Rider (1976)	CKE, SDA, PSA	$M(t)/M(t)/1$	$E[L^S(t)], P_0(t)$
Upton and Tripathi (1982)	BOT, DTA	$M(t)/M/1$	$E[L^S(t)]$
Ong and Taaffe (1988)	CKE, SDA	$PH(t)/PH(t)/1/K$	$E[L^S(t)], SD[L^S(t)]$
Taaffe and Clark (1988)	CKE, SDA	$M(t)/M/1/K/NPPrio$	$E[L^S(t)]$
Brilon and Wu (1990)	CTT, DTA	$M(t)/D/1$	$E[L^Q(t)]$
Tipper and Sundareshan (1990)	CKE, PSFFA	$M(t)/M/1$	$E[L^Q(t)]$
Choudhury et al. (1997)	BOT, SIPP	$M(t)/G(t)/1$	$E[\text{Workload}(t)]$
Czachórski et al. (2009)	CKE, DIFF	$M(t)/M/1/K/PPrio$	$E[L^S(t)], P_0(t), P_K(t)$
Viti and van Zuylen (2009)	DTA, FLUID	$M(t)/D(t)/1/K$	$E[L^S(t)], SD[L^S(t)]$
Viti and van Zuylen (2010)	DTA, FLUID	$M(t)/D(t)/1/K$	$E[L^S(t)], SD[L^S(t)]$
Multi-server queueing systems ($1 \leq c < \infty$)			
Rothkopf and Oren (1979)	CKE, SDA	$M(t)/M/c$	$E[L^S(t)], SD[L^S(t)]$
Clark (1981)	CKE, SDA	$M(t)/M/c$	$E[L^S(t)], \text{Var}[L^S(t)], E[W^Q(t)]$
Sze (1984)	SIPP, MOL	$M(t)/G/c$	$E[W^Q(t)]$
Taaffe and Ong (1987)	CKE, SDA	$PH(t)/M(t)/c/k$	$E[L^S(t)], SD[L^S(t)]$
Jung and Lee (1989a)	DIFF, FLUID	$G(t)/G/c(t)$	$E[L^S(t)]$
Green and Kolesar (1991)	CKE, PSA, SSA	$M(t)/M/c$	$E[L^Q(t)], P_w(t)$
Green et al. (1991)	CKE, SSA	$M(t)/M/c$	$E[L^Q(t)], E[W^Q(t)], P_w(t)$
Green and Kolesar (1995)	CKE, PSA, SPHA	$M(t)/M/c$	$P_w(t), E[W^Q(t)]$
Green and Kolesar (1997)	CKE, INFSA, Lagged PSA, SPEA	$M(t)/M/c$	$P_w(t)$

Table 2.11: cont.

Reference	Compared methods	Queueing system	Performance measures
Massey and Whitt (1997)	CKE, MOL	$M(t)/M/c$	$P_w(t)$, $\mathrm{E}[W^Q(t)]$
Green et al. (2001)	SIPP avg/max/mix, Lag avg/max/mix	$M(t)/M/c(t)$	$P_w(t)$
Ingolfsson et al. (2002)	CKE, SIPP	$M(t)/M/c(t)/K$	$P_w(t)$
Ingolfsson et al. (2007)	CKE, INFSA, Lag avg, MOL, SDA, UR	$M(t)/M/c(t)$	$P(W^Q \le \alpha)(t)$
Wall and Worthington (2007)	DTA, PSA, SSA	$M(t)/G/c$	$\mathrm{E}[W^Q(t)]$, $\mathrm{Quant}^{0.95}[W^Q(t)]$
Whitt (2007)	PSA, Lagged PSA, MOL	$M(t)/M/c(t)+M$	$\mathrm{E}[L^S(t)]$, $P_w(t)$
Atlason et al. (2008)	SIPP avg/max/mix, Lag avg/max/mix	$M(t)/M/c(t)$	$P_w(t)$
Stolletz (2008a)	SBC, SIPP	$M(t)/M(t)/c(t)$	$\mathrm{E}[U(t)]$, $\mathrm{E}[L^S(t)]$, $\mathrm{E}[L^Q(t)]$
Stolletz (2011)	FLUID, SBC, SIPP	$M(t)/G/c(t)$	$\mathrm{E}[U(t)]$, $\mathrm{E}[L^Q(t)]$, $\mathrm{E}[W^Q(t)]$
Chen et al. (2013)	PSFFA, SBC	$M(t)/E_k/c$	$\mathrm{E}[L^Q(t)]$
Massey and Pender (2013)	FLUID, DIFF, SDA	$M(t)/M/c(t)+M$	$\mathrm{E}[L^S(t)]$, $\mathrm{Var}[L^S(t)]$
Chen and Yang (2014a)	FLUID, PSA, PSFFA	$M(t)/G/c$	$\mathrm{E}[L^Q(t)]$
Pender (2014a)	FLUID, DIFF, SDA	$M(t)/M(t)/c(t)+M(t)$	$\mathrm{E}[L^S(t)]$, $\mathrm{Var}[L^S(t)]$
Selinka et al. (2016)	SBC, SIPP	$M(t)/M/c$	$\mathrm{E}[U(t)]$, $\mathrm{E}[L^S(t)]$, $\mathrm{E}[L^Q(t)]$, $\mathrm{E}[W^Q(t)]$

Infinite-server queueing systems ($c = \infty$)

Reference	Compared methods	Queueing system	Performance measures
Eick et al. (1993a)	EXPL, PSA, SSA	$M(t)/G/\infty$	$\mathrm{E}[L^S(t)]$
Green and Kolesar (1998)	EXPL, SPEA, SPHA	$M(t)/G/\infty$	$\mathrm{E}[L^S(t)]$
Pang and Whitt (2012b)	PSA, RA	$M(t)/G^D/\infty$	$\mathrm{Var}[L^S(t)]$

2.5 Areas of application

2.5.1 Service systems

Many customer service systems experience time-dependent arrival rates and numbers of servers (Thompson (1993), Whitt (2013)). Surveys on time-dependent queueing models that are used for staffing decisions in service systems are provided by Green et al. (2007), Whitt (2007), Defraeye and Van Nieuwenhuyse (2011), and Defraeye and Van Nieuwenhuyse (2016). Hampshire and Massey (2010) integrate the performance analysis of time-dependent queueing systems in the optimization of multiple aspects of the communications industry. The applications can be categorized into the areas of telephone call centers, health care facilities, emergency services, service counters, and repair facilities.

Inbound **telephone call centers** are often characterized by a time-dependent arrival rate and a time-dependent number of agents (Gans et al. (2003)). Whereas Sze (1984), Aguir et al. (2004), and Ridley et al. (2004) describe the performance evaluation of call centers, all other references cited in this paragraph concentrate on the development of staffing algorithms for call centers. Kolesar and Green (1998) focus on the analysis of the peak hour in their staffing analysis. Most of the models for call centers apply queueing systems with Poisson arrivals and exponentially distributed service times (Andrews and Parsons (1993), Kolesar and Green (1998), Green et al. (2001), Green et al. (2003), Koole and van der Sluis (2003), Ridley et al. (2004), Dietz and Vaver (2006), Atlason et al. (2008), Hampshire et al. (2009), Ingolfsson et al. (2010)). Abandonments are considered by Feldman et al. (2008), Hampshire et al. (2009), Bertsimas and Doan (2010), Dietz (2011), and Kim and Ha (2012). Customers who reenter the system after abandonment (retrials) are analyzed by Sze (1984) and Aguir et al. (2004). Sze (1984) considers abandonments as part of the arriving jobs that require a service time of zero. All of the models mentioned above consider systems with an infinite waiting room. In contrast, Mok and Shanthikumar (1987) consider a system with a limited waiting room. A call center that can be modeled as an $M(t, n)/G/c$ queueing system with state-dependent balking is considered by Chassioti et al. (2014). Mok and Shanthikumar (1987) consider a heterogeneous queueing system with two server classes, i.e., scheduled servers and standby servers that are used only if the queue exceeds a predetermined threshold. Different job classes and job class-dependent priorities are considered by Ridley et al. (2004) and Bertsimas and Doan (2010).

The request for medical services at **health care** facilities, such as emergency departments, can vary significantly over time (Bhattacharjee and Ray (2014)). Consequently, the number of medical personnel is often also time-dependent. Applications include the performance analysis of emergency facilities (Collings and Stoneman (1976), De Bruin et al. (2007)), staffing in clinical wards (Agnihothri and Taylor (1991), Gillard and Knight (2014), Yom-Tov and Mandelbaum (2014)), and ambulance management (Singer and Donoso (2008)). Yom-Tov and Mandelbaum (2014) derive a model that includes re-entrant patients/repetitive service in clinical wards. Brahimi and Worthington (1991a) and Bennett and Worthington (1998) use the DTA to analyze out-patient appointment systems. The optimal patient mix with respect to patient service requirements is analyzed by Vanberkel et al. (2014).

Similarly, **emergency services** providers, such as police or fire fighters, face time-dependent service requests. Such systems are considered in the staffing and scheduling algorithm of Green et al. (2006). Green and Kolesar (1995) evaluate peak hour effects for emergency service systems. Bookbinder and Martell (1979) minimize the damage potential of forest fires by considering the allocation of available helicopters. Alfa and Margolius (2008) evaluate the queue of requests for police patrol cars, and Kolesar et al. (1975) and Ingolfsson et al. (2002) apply time-dependent queueing systems as part of scheduling algorithms for police patrol cars.

Service counters and facilities in airport terminals, such as check-in counters, security checks, departure lounges, and baggage claim facilities, experience time-dependent traveler arrivals. A detailed description of these applications is provided in the survey by Tošić (1992). The approaches of Horonjeff (1969), Paullin and Horonjeff (1969), de Neufville and Grillot (1982), Wirasinghe and Shehata (1988), Wirasinghe and Bandara (1990), and De Barros and Tomber (2007) rely on the fluid approximation. Stolletz (2011) uses the SBC to analyze the performance of check-in counters. As another type of service counter with time-dependent arrivals, a fast food restaurant is studied by Kwan et al. (1988). Foote (1976) evaluates the performance of a drive-in banking facility with multiple lines involving jockeying. Kolesar (1984) analyzes the expected number of waiting customers in front of automated teller machines to evaluate different layouts for a bank lobby. The staffing at border crossings in the form of a stationary congestion-based policy is considered by Zhang (2009). Liu and Wein (2008) derive a model to determine the number of necessary beds for the detention and removal of illegal aliens at border crossings.

The demand for repairs at **repair facilities** is also often time-dependent. The analysis of such systems provides insights into the required inventory level of spare parts over time. Jung (1993) analyzes a repair facility for expensive aircraft parts. Jung and Lee (1989a) and Lau and Song (2008) optimize stocking levels of spare parts in repair facilities in a military context. Buczkowski and Kulkarni (2006) use the explicit solution of an $M(t)/G/\infty$ system to model the time-dependent number of items under warranty to determine the optimal funding of a warranty reserve.

All references reporting an application in the area of service systems are listed in Table 2.12. The second column (Embedded) shows that the performance evaluation is often embedded within optimization algorithms, especially for call centers and emergency services. The third column indicates whether real-world data are used in the numerical study. The fluid approximation and methods based on stationary models are most frequently used.

Table 2.12: Applications in the area of service systems

Reference	Embedded	Real data	Eval. method
Telephone call centers			
Sze (1984)			SIPP
Mok and Shanthikumar (1987)	x	x	UR
Andrews and Parsons (1993)	x	x	SIPP
Kolesar and Green (1998)	x	x	SPHA
Green et al. (2001)	x	x	SIPP
Green et al. (2003)	x	x	SIPP
Koole and van der Sluis (2003)	x	x	SIPP
Aguir et al. (2004)		x	FLUID
Ridley et al. (2004)		x	FLUID
Dietz and Vaver (2006)	x		SIPP
Atlason et al. (2008)	x		SIPP
Feldman et al. (2008)	x		INFSA, MOL
Hampshire et al. (2009)	x		FLUID
Bertsimas and Doan (2010)	x	x	FLUID
Ingolfsson et al. (2010)	x		SIPP, UR
Dietz (2011)	x	x	SIPP
Kim and Ha (2012)	x	x	EXPL
Chassioti et al. (2014)	x		PSA
Health care			
Collings and Stoneman (1976)			EXPL
Agnihothri and Taylor (1991)	x	x	SIPP
Brahimi and Worthington (1991a)		x	DTA
Bennett and Worthington (1998)		x	DTA
De Bruin et al. (2007)		x	SIPP
Singer and Donoso (2008)		x	SIPP
Gillard and Knight (2014)	x		CKE
Vanberkel et al. (2014)	x	x	PSA
Yom-Tov and Mandelbaum (2014)	x	x	MOL
Emergency services			
Kolesar et al. (1975)	x	x	CKE, SIPP
Bookbinder and Martell (1979)	x	x	CKE
Green and Kolesar (1995)			SPHA
Ingolfsson et al. (2002)	x	x	CKE, SIPP
Green et al. (2006)	x	x	SIPP
Alfa and Margolius (2008)		x	DTA
Service counters			
Horonjeff (1969)		x	FLUID
Paullin and Horonjeff (1969)		x	FLUID
Foote (1976)		x	SIPP
de Neufville and Grillot (1982)		x	FLUID
Kolesar (1984)		x	SIPP
Kwan et al. (1988)	x	x	SIPP
Wirasinghe and Shehata (1988)	x		FLUID

Reference	Embedded	Real data	Eval. method
Wirasinghe and Bandara (1990)	x	x	FLUID
Thompson (1993)	x		SIPP
De Barros and Tomber (2007)		x	FLUID
Liu and Wein (2008)		x	MOL, PSA
Zhang (2009)			SIPP
Stolletz (2011)			SBC
Repair facilities			
Jung and Lee (1989a)	x		DIFF, FLUID
Jung (1993)	x		CKE
Buczkowski and Kulkarni (2006)	x		EXPL
Lau and Song (2008)	x		SDA

2.5.2 Road and air traffic systems

Road traffic systems, such as roads, bridges, and intersections, are often analyzed by using time-dependent queueing systems to model rush hour and off-peak effects in traffic flows. Catling (1977) applies the CTT for an $M(t)/G/1$ system to analyze the delay at road junctions. The same approximation method is used by Kimber et al. (1977), Kimber and Hollis (1978), and Kimber and Daly (1986) to analyze the performance of three-arm major/minor priority junctions. Kimber et al. (1977) and Kimber and Hollis (1978) apply an $M(t)/M(t)/1$ model and restrict their analysis to artificial data, whereas Kimber and Daly (1986) consider real-world data and apply a $G(t)/G(t)/1$ system. The CTT is applied by Griffiths et al. (1991) to analyze the Channel Tunnel between France and England modeled as an $M(t)/G^{(0,s)}/1$ system. Brilon and Wu (1990) compare the results of a discrete-time approach with empirical data for a one-lane street with a traffic light. Viti and van Zuylen (2009) and Viti and van Zuylen (2010) develop a DTA to evaluate the queue length at the end of and within a green/red cycle of intersections. Blumberg-Nitzani and Bar-Gera (2014) obtain within-cycle results through an interpolation between the results of the end-of-cycle model. Griffiths et al. (2008) analyze a 24-hour flow pattern on the Severn Bridge between England and Wales as an $M(t)/E_k/1$ system based on piecewise transient models. Gaver (1969) applies the fluid approximation to analyze the time-dependent queueing delays that occur during and after accidents on freeways. Departure time choice and commuting problems also often rely on the deterministic fluid approximation (see Kuwahara (2007) and the references therein).

Time-dependent demand is also distinct for **car and truck handling facilities**. Chen and Yang (2010), Chen et al. (2011), Chen et al. (2013), Chen et al. (2013), Chen et al. (2013), Yang et al. (2013), and Chen and Yang (2014) analyze truck handling facilities at seaports. Based on these analyses, several optimization techniques are proposed to optimize the time-dependent truck arrival process. Selinka et al. (2016) apply the SBC to the performance evaluation of the truck handling system at an air cargo hub with heterogeneous jobs and heterogeneous servers.

Curry et al. (1978) analyze the performance of the queueing process at an airport's taxi stand. In their analysis, they consider the exponentially distributed clearing of a queue that corresponds to a context in which busses collect all customers waiting for a taxi. Deng et al. (1992) develop a model for the optimal allocation of taxis to service zones.

Air traffic is also often time-dependent. Early models for the analysis of runways are proposed by Galliher and Wheeler (1958), Koopman (1972), and Omosigho and Worthington (1985). Bookbinder (1986) analyzes a Markovian queueing system with two separate queues for landing and departing aircrafts and a single runway as a common server. Stolletz (2008b) analyzes a similar model with generally distributed service times. Hebert and Dietz (1997) use the uniformization/randomization approximation and Lovell et al. (2013) use the diffusion approximation to evaluate the time dependent performance of a single runway. Janic (2009) investigates delays on airport runways under heavy snowfall. In the analysis, the runway's service rate depends on a second queue representing the accumulated snow at airports. Jacquillat and Odoni (2015) use a queueing model in their algorithm to control departure and arrival service rates to maximize the efficiency of an airport's runway system.

Jung and Lee (1989b) propose a dynamic programming approach with an embedded time-dependent queueing model to staff air traffic controllers. Congestion-based prices for airport capacity are determined based on the diffusion approximation by Janic (2005), whereas Daniel (1995), Daniel and Pahwa (2000), Daniel and Harback (2008), and Daniel and Harback (2009) use the basic DTA of Galliher and Wheeler (1958). Swaroop et al. (2012) include the fluid approximation in their derivation of slot-controlled flight schedules.

Table 2.13: Applications in the areas of road and air traffic

Reference	Embedded	Real data	Eval. method
Road traffic			
Gaver (1969)			FLUID
Catling (1977)			CTT
Kimber et al. (1977)			CTT
Kimber and Hollis (1978)			CTT
Kimber and Daly (1986)		x	CTT
Brilon and Wu (1990)		x	DTA
Griffiths et al. (1991)			CTT
Kuwahara (2007)	x		FLUID
Griffiths et al. (2008)		x	BOT
Viti and van Zuylen (2009)			DTA, FLUID
Viti and van Zuylen (2010)			DTA, FLUID
Blumberg-Nitzani and Bar-Gera (2014)			DTA
Car and truck handling facilities			
Curry et al. (1978)		x	SIPP
Deng et al. (1992)	x	x	SIPP
Chen and Yang (2010)	x		FLUID
Chen et al. (2011)	x		PSFFA
Chen et al. (2013)	x	x	PSFFA
Chen et al. (2013)	x	x	PSFFA
Chen et al. (2013)	x		PSFFA
Yang et al. (2013)	x		PSFFA
Chen and Yang (2014)		x	FLUID, PSA, PSFFA
Selinka et al. (2016)		x	SBC
Air traffic			
Galliher and Wheeler (1958)		x	DTA
Koopman (1972)		x	CKE, DTA, FLUID
Omosigho and Worthington (1985)		x	DTA
Bookbinder (1986)		x	CKE
Jung and Lee (1989b)	x		CKE
Daniel (1995)	x	x	DTA
Hebert and Dietz (1997)		x	BOT
Daniel and Pahwa (2000)	x	x	DTA

Table 2.13: cont.

Reference	Embedded	Real data	Eval. method
Janic (2005)	x	x	DIFF
Daniel and Harback (2008)	x	x	DTA
Stolletz (2008b)			SBC
Daniel and Harback (2009)	x	x	DTA
Janic (2009)		x	FLUID
Swaroop et al. (2012)	x	x	FLUID
Lovell et al. (2013)		x	DIFF
Jacquillat and Odoni (2015)	x	x	CKE

All references considered in this section are included in Table 2.13. The number of servers in road and air traffic systems cannot be adjusted over time. Instead, arrival patterns are optimized, e.g., at truck handling facilities.

2.5.3 IT systems

Computer and communication networks transfer data packets whose arrival rates often significantly vary over time (Tripathi and Duda (1986)). The amount of data that can be stored at a certain node is limited. Full buffers may lead to serious performance degradations owing to delays from waiting for transmission capacity or packet retransmissions. Lackman et al. (1992) develop a DTA for a statistical multiplexer that processes real-time and non-real-time traffic. Van As (1986) compares a common-buffer configuration with a foreground-background congestion control mechanism. Tipper and Sundareshan (1990) demonstrate how the PSFFA can be used to find optimal time-dependent arrival rates to individual nodes. The PSFFA is also used by Xu et al. (2014) to evaluate the performance of nodes in multihop wireless networks with constant bit rate traffic. Czachórski et al. (2009) and Czachórski et al. (2010) use the diffusion approximation to model nodes in a wireless network based on the IEEE 802.11 standard and the impact of an adaptive increase and decrease in TCP flow. The fluid and diffusion approximations are used by Ko and Gautam (2010) for the performance evaluation of queues that occur for peer-based multimedia content delivery. The number of active nodes of two different classes in a peer-to-peer (P2P) internet telephony system is modeled with an $M(t)/M/\infty$ system and analyzed via the SIPP and explicit solutions by Kuraya et al. (2009) and Kuraya et al. (2011). McCalla and Whitt (2002) evaluate the volume of lines in private line telecommunication services by using the explicit solution of a $G(t)^{X(t)}/G(t)/\infty$ system.

Rothkopf and Johnston (1982) apply the SDA to predict the queues in front of printers for which the arrival rate of jobs is time-dependent. The coverage process on a straight line in a sensor field is analyzed by Manohar et al. (2009), who show that this process can be modeled as a time-dependent $M(t)/G(t)/\infty$ system. In such a system, the time corresponds to the location in the sensor field, and the number of jobs in the system corresponds to the number of sensors that cover the associated area.

All references reporting applications with IT systems are presented in Table 2.14. In contrast to studies on other areas of application, most references focus on the performance evaluation only.

Table 2.14: Applications in the area of IT systems

Reference	Embedded	Real data	Eval. method
Rothkopf and Johnston (1982)		x	SDA
Van As (1986)			CKE
Tipper and Sundareshan (1990)	x		PSFFA
Lackman et al. (1992)			DTA
McCalla and Whitt (2002)		x	EXPL
Kuraya et al. (2009)			SIPP
Czachórski et al. (2009)			DIFF
Manohar et al. (2009)			PSA
Czachórski et al. (2010)			DIFF
Ko and Gautam (2010)			DIFF, FLUID
Kuraya et al. (2011)			EXPL
Xu et al. (2014)			PSFFA

2.6 Conclusions and future research

This paper provides a structured overview of approaches for the performance evaluation of time-dependent queueing systems (Section 2.3). We discuss links between the different approaches and demonstrate that numerical comparisons exist only for a subset of the existing approaches (Section 2.4). Thus, a research gap remains for a comprehensive numerical study comparing the approximation quality of approaches within all three categories for different types of queueing systems with various levels of stochasticity and different time-dependent patterns for the system parameters. Moreover, a methodological extension of some approaches is needed to analyze general systems. An opportunity for the development of new approaches lies in the combination of existing ideas concerning approximation. For instance, a transformation, as suggested by the CTT, could be integrated into approaches that currently rely on regular steady-state queueing formulas.

Section 2.5 demonstrates the wide range of areas of application for time-dependent queueing systems, including service, road and air traffic, and IT systems. The currently used evaluation methods are often based on stationary models, discrete-time approaches, or fluid approximations. Notably, some evaluation methods are used only within a single area of application. For example, the CTT is used only for the analysis of road traffic systems, and the PSFFA is used mainly for truck handling facilities. In general, for all areas of application, a systematic test of other evaluation approaches may represent a worthwhile investigation. Most of the optimization algorithms that use embedded time-dependent queueing formulas involve decisions regarding the number of servers in service systems. In the area of truck handling and IT systems, the arrival rate is treated as a decision variable. The optimization of service rates is addressed only by the theoretical work of Parlar (1984) and is a potential field of future research. Another open field is the time-dependent decision regarding the provision of waiting rooms, which is introduced in a call center context by

Hampshire et al. (2009). In summary, this review shows that there are numerous areas of application for time-dependent queues. A promising field of research is the extensive use of time-dependent performance evaluation approaches as embedded with optimization procedures.

3 Time-dependent performance approximation of truck handling operations at an air cargo terminal

Co-authors:

Axel Franz
Center for Doctoral Studies in Business, Graduate School of Economic
& Social Sciences, University of Mannheim, Germany

Raik Stolletz
Chair of Production Management, Business School, University of
Mannheim, Germany

Published as:

Selinka, G., A. Franz, and R. Stolletz (2014): Time-dependent
performance approximation of truck handling operations at an air cargo
terminal. *Computers & Operations Research 65*, 164-173.

Abstract:

This paper provides an analytical solution for the time-dependent performance evaluation of truck handling operations at an air cargo terminal. The demand for loading and unloading operations is highly time-
dependent and stochastic for two classes of trucks. Two heterogeneous
handling facilities with multiple servers are available to handle trucks as-

suming exponentially distributed processing times. Trucks are routed to a handling facility depending on the current state of the system upon arrival. To approximate the time-dependent behavior of such heterogeneous queueing systems, we develop a stationary backlog-carryover (SBC) approach. A numerical study compares this approach with simulations and demonstrates its applicability to real-world input data.

3.1 Introduction

The demand for air cargo transportation services is cyclical in nature. On the one hand, this demand is characterized by strong interdependencies between the economic situation and long-term airfreight volumes (Kasarda and Green (2005)). On the other hand, considerable peaks and off-peaks in air cargo transportation activities occur within a day (Leleu and Marsh (2009)). These dynamics are reflected in the demand for freight handling capacity at air cargo terminals. Air cargo terminals serve as cross-docking facilities for sorting, (re-)consolidation, and short-term storage before and after transportation by air (e.g., Rong and Grunow (2009)). Airfreight shipments are delivered and picked up by trucks (e.g., Ou et al. (2010)). Such road transportation takes a fundamental position in the air cargo logistics chain. Freight forwarders provide trucking services for air cargo shipments from the shipper to the origin airport and from the destination airport to the consignee (e.g., Wan et al. (1998)). Furthermore, cargo airlines themselves operate scheduled intra-continental road feeder services between airports in their hub-and-spoke networks (e.g., Bartodziej et al. (2009)). Especially within Europe, such trucking services have increased significantly at an annual growth rate of 20% between 2002 and 2012, amounting to nearly 20,000 scheduled intra-European frequencies per week (Crabtree et al. (2012)).

In this paper, we analyze the truck handling operations at the hub of one of Europe's largest combination carriers. An evaluation of such a system's time-dependent performance provides crucial information for various managerial decisions. Operations managers of air cargo terminals have to evaluate the time-dependent operational performance to adjust capacity levels, to change operational handling procedures, and (if possible) to schedule truck arrivals. Thus far, the performance of air cargo operations (e.g., Lee et al. (2006), Ou et al. (2007)) and of truck handling operations in other contexts (e.g., Haughton and Sapna Isotupa (2012), Haughton and Isotupa (2013) under non-stationary conditions has mainly been analyzed by simulation. The objective of this work is to develop and evaluate an accurate and fast analytical approximation method for the time-dependent performance evaluation of truck handling operations at an air cargo terminal.

The corresponding system features two handling facilities for loading and unloading activities of unit load devices (ULDs), such as pallets and containers used for consolidated transportation. While facility 1 is equipped with a single truck dock, facility 2 features two parallel truck docks. Because of different operational requirements, such as requirements regarding shape, size, and weight, we distinguish two heterogeneous classes of trucks according to the type of airfreight carried: (1) Export deliveries, which can be handled only at handling facility 1, and (2) import and transit shipments, which can be handled at both facilities. The number of truck arrivals is highly time-dependent, resulting in significant variations in activity level throughout a day with peaks typically occurring at night. Such fluctuations are somewhat predictable, the actual extent, however, is subject to uncertainty. Processing times are stochastic and facility-dependent, but independent of the truck class, as empirical analyses revealed. We assume that the processing times are time-independent. Since the two handling facilities lie some distance apart, arriving trucks are assigned to one of the available facilities upon arrival. Trucks with export shipments are exclusively routed to handling facility 1. For trucks with import or transit shipments, the routing decision depends on the current numbers of trucks being handled or waiting at each handling facility. Trucks waiting for cargo handling services are processed on a first-come, first-served basis at both facilities.

Similar queueing systems with heterogeneous servers and heterogeneous jobs which join a queue directly upon arrival have been analyzed in steady state only prior to this study. Static routing decisions are analyzed by Ross and Yao (1991), Ansell et al. (2003), Argon et al. (2009), and Liu and Righter (1998). In the case of state-dependent routing, threshold policies based on a particular facility may be applied (e.g., Schwartz (1974), Teh and Ward (2002)) or routing decisions may be based on the state of several stations; e.g., an arriving job may be routed to the facility with the shortest queue (e.g., Foschini and Salz (1978), Akgun et al. (2012)). Furthermore, in contrast to our setting, all of these references primarily restrict the scope of analysis to parallel single-server queues. The term "N-system" is often used to describe similar queueing systems in call centers. However, while trucks are routed directly at arrival in the considered truck handling system, calls are routed just before being served in call center systems, but wait in job specific queues (e.g., Gans et al. (2003), Garnett and Mandelbaum (2000)).

There exist different approaches for the non-stationary analysis of homogeneous queueing systems. The numerical solution of the respective set of ordinary differential equations (e.g., Koopman (1972), Odoni and Roth (1983)) and the randomization approach (Gross and Miller (1984)) are applicable to Markovian systems. Although these methods provide (nearly) exact results, the numerical solution is rather time-consuming (Ingolfsson et al. (2007)). Deterministic fluid approaches approximate discrete events through continuous processes. These approaches are fast and suitable for the time-dependent analysis of overloaded systems (e.g., Newell (1971), Janic (2009)). However, any queue in an underloaded system is not considered. Another class of approximations is based upon the application of steady-state models. Comparing various approximation methods, Ingolfsson et al. (2007) show that the stationary independent period-by-period (SIPP) approximation achieves good results within a reasonable time. This method divides the observed time horizon into multiple smaller periods and then analyzes each period independently using a stationary model (Green et al. (2001)). In contrast, the stationary backlog-carryover (SBC) approach considers the dependencies between successive periods (Stolletz (2008a)). This method builds backlogs of non-served arrivals and carries them over to the succeeding period. Numerical studies indicate better approximation results than the SIPP approach for $M(t)/M/c(t)$ systems.

The contribution of this paper is the analysis of a queueing system with two heterogeneous classes of trucks, two separate handling facilities with multiple servers, and state-dependent routing upon arrival. Based on a stationary Markov model, we develop an SBC approach for the time-dependent performance evaluation. The approximation method is applied to arbitrary state-dependent routing policies.

The remainder of this paper is organized as follows. Section 3.2 introduces the queueing model of the analyzed truck handling system. The corresponding Markov chain and the calculation of the steady-state performance are presented in Section 3.3. The first part of Section 3.4 provides a brief introduction to the SIPP approach to analyze non-stationary systems. The SBC approach for the heterogeneous queueing system is developed in the second part of Section 3.4. In Section 3.5, a numerical study is conducted for the purpose of comparing the SIPP and SBC approximations with simulation results. Furthermore, a sensitivity analysis with respect to handling capacities, demand, and routing policies is presented to gain insights into the real-world behavior of the system. A conclusion and suggestions for further research are provided in Section 3.6.

3.2 The queueing model

The truck handling system is represented by a queueing model with heterogeneous jobs (i.e., truck classes), with heterogeneous servers (i.e., truck docks) at two parallel stations (i.e., handling facilities), and with routing decisions before entering a queue (see Figure 3.1).

We distinguish between two independent inhomogeneous Poisson arrival processes with instantaneous arrival rates $\lambda_A(t)$ and $\lambda_B(t)$, respectively. Trucks of class A carry export shipments, whereas trucks of class B are dedicated to import and transit shipments. Depending on the truck handling facility, the servers represent flexible or specialized truck docks for loading and unloading activities. Handling facility 1 features c_1 flexible

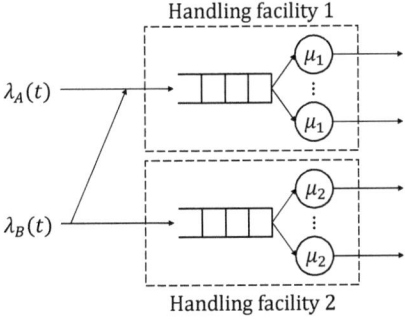

Figure 3.1: The model of the truck handling system

servers, which are able to handle trucks of classes A and B. Handling facility 2 is equipped with c_2 parallel specialized truck docks, which are only able to handle trucks of class B. The truck docks are assumed to operate with exponentially distributed service times at constant rates μ_1 and μ_2 independent of truck class. There is a single queue in front of each handling facility which is served on a first-come, first-served basis. We assume an infinitely large waiting room.

The state of the system is described by a tuple (n_1, n_2), where n_1 denotes the overall number of trucks at facility 1, i.e., the trucks being processed at a server or waiting, and where n_2 denotes the overall number of trucks at facility 2. All possible states are included in the infinite state space:

$$\mathcal{S} = \{(n_1, n_2)|n_1 \in \{0, 1, 2, ...\}; n_2 \in \{0, 1, 2, ...\}\} \qquad (3.1)$$

Immediately upon arrival, trucks are assigned to one of the two handling facilities. An arriving truck of class A is always served at handling facility 1, whereas a truck of class B can be handled at either facility. Let $R(n_1, n_2)$ define the state-dependent routing decision for an arriving class

67

B truck, i.e.,

$$R(n_1, n_2) = \begin{cases} 1, & \text{if an arriving truck of class } B \text{ is routed} \\ & \text{to the flexible facility 1,} \\ 0, & \text{if an arriving truck of class } B \text{ is routed} \\ & \text{to the specialized facility 2.} \end{cases} \tag{3.2}$$

For example, in the truck handling system at the considered air cargo hub, an arriving truck of class B is routed to handling facility 1 if the following two conditions are met:

- There is no server available at specialized handling facility 2.

- The ratio of the numbers of trucks at handling facilities 1 and 2 is smaller than a predefined parameter ω.

This results in the following definition of the routing decision:

$$R_\omega(n_1, n_2) = \begin{cases} 1, & \text{if} \quad n_2 \geq c_2 \quad \wedge \quad n_1 < \omega \cdot n_2, \\ 0, & \text{otherwise} \end{cases} \tag{3.3}$$

The idea behind the first condition of the routing policy $R_\omega(n_1, n_2)$ is to prioritize handling facility 2 as long as there are idle truck docks available. The second condition takes the ratio of the current numbers of trucks at both facilities into account. One possibility to define ω is to relate the overall processing rates of the two handling facilities to each other, i.e., $\omega = (c_1 \cdot \mu_1)/(c_2 \cdot \mu_2)$.

Performance measures of interest are the expected time-dependent number of trucks at each facility, $\mathrm{E}[L_1^S(t)]$ and $\mathrm{E}[L_2^S(t)]$; the expected times in the system for trucks arriving at time t, $\mathrm{E}[W_1^S(t)]$ and $\mathrm{E}[W_2^S(t)]$; the expected number of waiting trucks, $\mathrm{E}[L_1^Q(t)]$ and $\mathrm{E}[L_2^Q(t)]$; the expected waiting times for trucks arriving at time t, $\mathrm{E}[W_1^Q(t)]$ and $\mathrm{E}[W_2^Q(t)]$; and the expected utilizations, $\mathrm{E}[U_1(t)]$ and $\mathrm{E}[U_2(t)]$.

3.3 Steady-state performance

As the inter-arrival times for each truck class and the processing times at both facilities are exponentially distributed, the system's behavior can be modeled by a continuous-time Markov chain. To derive a finite state space, we assume that the overall number of trucks at facility 1 may not exceed K_1 trucks and that the system size of facility 2 is restricted to K_2 trucks ($K_1 \geq c_1$, $K_2 \geq c_2$). The modified state space is given by

$$\mathcal{S}^* = \{(n_1, n_2) | n_1 \in \{0, 1, 2, ..., K_1\}; n_2 \in \{0, 1, 2, ..., K_2\}\}. \quad (3.4)$$

To calculate the steady-state probabilities $P_{(n_1, n_2)}$, the Chapman-Kolmogorov equation has to be derived for every state $(n_1, n_2) \in \mathcal{S}^*$ (Eq. (3.5)).

$$
\begin{aligned}
&\lambda_A \cdot P_{(n_1, n_2)} \cdot \mathbf{1}_{[n_1 < K_1]} \\
&+ \lambda_B \cdot P_{(n_1, n_2)} \cdot \mathbf{1}_{[(n_1 < K_1 \wedge R(n_1, n_2) = 1) \vee (n_2 < K_2 \wedge R(n_1, n_2) = 0)]} \\
&+ \min\{n_1, c_1\} \cdot \mu_1 \cdot P_{(n_1, n_2)} \\
&+ \min\{n_2, c_2\} \cdot \mu_2 \cdot P_{(n_1, n_2)} \\
= &\ \lambda_B \cdot P_{(n_1, n_2 - 1)} \cdot \mathbf{1}_{[n_2 - 1 \geq 0 \wedge R(n_1, n_2 - 1) = 0]} \\
&+ (\lambda_A + \lambda_B \cdot \mathbf{1}_{[R(n_1 - 1, n_2) = 1]}) \cdot P_{(n_1 - 1, n_2)} \cdot \mathbf{1}_{[n_1 - 1 \geq 0]} \\
&+ \min\{n_2 + 1, c_2\} \cdot \mu_2 \cdot P_{(n_1, n_2 + 1)} \cdot \mathbf{1}_{[n_2 < K_2]} \\
&+ \min\{n_1 + 1, c_1\} \cdot \mu_1 \cdot P_{(n_1 + 1, n_2)} \cdot \mathbf{1}_{[n_1 < K_1]} \quad (3.5)
\end{aligned}
$$

The total outflow rate out of state (n_1, n_2) includes truck arrivals and trucks leaving the system. Arriving trucks enter the system only if the assigned facility is not full. Otherwise, they are lost and their arrival does not result in a state transition. An arrival of a truck of class A occurs at rate λ_A and has to be considered if there is available waiting space at facility 1, i.e., $n_1 < K_1$ holds. Trucks of class B reach the system at rate λ_B. These trucks are either handled at facility 1 or at facility 2, depending on the state of the system. In case $R(n_1, n_2) = 1$, an arriving truck of class B is routed to facility 1 and thus must be considered if facility 1 is not fully occupied, i.e., $n_1 < K_1$ holds. When $R(n_1, n_2) = 0$ is fulfilled, an arriving truck of class B is routed to facility 2, if there is waiting space available at facility 2, i.e., $n_2 < K_2$ holds. Therefore, a truck arrival of class B has to be taken into account if the condition $(n_1 < K_1 \wedge R(n_1, n_2) = 1) \vee (n_2 < K_2 \wedge R(n_1, n_2) = 0)$ holds. As facility 1 works at processing rate μ_1, trucks leave facility 1 at rate $\min\{n_1, c_1\} \cdot \mu_1$. Trucks of class B leave facility 2 at rate $\min\{n_2, c_2\} \cdot \mu_2$.

The total inflow rate into state (n_1, n_2) includes a transition from state $(n_1, n_2 - 1)$. Such a transition occurs at rate λ_B and represents the arrival of a truck of class B that is routed to facility 2. This transition is possible if starting state $(n_1, n_2 - 1)$ exists, i.e., $n_2 - 1 \geq 0$ is fulfilled, and condition $R(n_1, n_2 - 1) = 0$ holds. A transition from state $(n_1 - 1, n_2)$ to state (n_1, n_2) occurs if an arriving truck is routed to facility 1. This transition includes truck arrivals of class A, which arrive at rate λ_A and which are always routed to facility 1, as well as arrivals of trucks of class B. However, an arrival of a truck of class B has to be taken into account only if the truck is routed to facility 1, i.e., condition $R(n_1 - 1, n_2) = 1$ is fulfilled. This transition has to be considered if the starting state exists, i.e., $n_1 - 1 \geq 0$ holds. A truck that is leaving facility 1 at rate μ_1 corresponds with a transition from state $(n_1 + 1, n_2)$ to state (n_1, n_2). This transition occurs at rate $\min\{n_1 + 1, c_1\} \cdot \mu_1$, if $n_1 + 1 \leq K_1$ holds. A transition from state $(n_1, n_2 + 1)$ to state (n_1, n_2) takes into account a service completion at facility 2.

The normalization equation (Eq. (3.6)) guarantees that the sum of all steady-state probabilities equals one.

$$\sum_{n_1=0}^{K_1} \sum_{n_2=0}^{K_2} P_{(n_1, n_2)} = 1 \qquad (3.6)$$

After solving the system of linear equations, the derived steady-state probabilities are used to calculate different performance measures. The expected utilization of handling facility 1 is given by Equation (3.7):

$$E[U_1] = \sum_{n_1=0}^{K_1} \sum_{n_2=0}^{K_2} \min\left\{\frac{n_1}{c_1}, 1\right\} \cdot P_{(n_1,n_2)} \tag{3.7}$$

The expected number of trucks at handling facility 1, which are either waiting or being served, is calculated by Equation (3.8):

$$E[L_1^S] = \sum_{n_1=0}^{K_1} \sum_{n_2=0}^{K_2} n_1 \cdot P_{(n_1,n_2)} \tag{3.8}$$

The effective arrival rate λ_1 at facility 1 is based on the arrivals of trucks of class A and the arrivals of trucks of class B that are routed to facility 1. An arriving truck of class B is routed to facility 1 if $R(n_1, n_2) = 1$ is fulfilled. Therefore, λ_1 can then be calculated by Equation (3.9):

$$\lambda_1 = \lambda_A + \lambda_B \cdot \sum_{n_1=0}^{K_1} \sum_{n_2=0}^{K_2} R(n_1, n_2) \cdot P_{(n_1,n_2)} \tag{3.9}$$

Little's law is applied to derive the expected time in the system per truck at handling facility 1 ($E[W_1^S]$) through Equation (3.10):

$$E[W_1^S] = \frac{E[L_1^S]}{\lambda_1} \tag{3.10}$$

The performance measures for handling facility 2 are calculated in a similar way using Equations (3.11) to (3.14):

$$E[U_2] = \sum_{n_1=0}^{K_1} \sum_{n_2=0}^{K_2} \min\left\{\frac{n_2}{c_2}, 1\right\} \cdot P_{(n_1,n_2)} \tag{3.11}$$

$$E[L_2^S] = \sum_{n_1=0}^{K_1} \sum_{n_2=0}^{K_2} n_2 \cdot P_{(n_1,n_2)} \tag{3.12}$$

$$\lambda_2 = \lambda_B \cdot \sum_{n_1=0}^{K_1} \sum_{n_2=0}^{K_2} (1 - R(n_1, n_2)) \cdot P_{(n_1, n_2)} \tag{3.13}$$

$$E\left[W_2^S\right] = \frac{E\left[L_2^S\right]}{\lambda_2} \tag{3.14}$$

In addition to facility related performance measures, the expected probability that an arriving truck of class A will be blocked, is calculated using Equation (3.15):

$$E\left[P_A^{block}\right] = \sum_{n_2=0}^{K_2} P_{(K_1, n_2)} \tag{3.15}$$

An arriving truck of class B is blocked from entering the system if the truck is routed to facility 1, i.e., $R(n_1, n_2) = 1$, and there is no waiting space available at facility 1, or if the truck is routed to facility 2, i.e., $R(n_1, n_2) = 0$, and there is no waiting space available at facility 2 (Eq. (3.16)).

$$E\left[P_B^{block}\right] = \sum_{n_2=0}^{K_2} R(K_1, n_2) \cdot P_{(K_1, n_2)}$$
$$+ \sum_{n_1=0}^{K_1} (1 - R(n_1, K_2)) \cdot P_{(n_1, K_2)} \tag{3.16}$$

In accordance with our specific real-world case, the truck handling system has $c_1 = 1$ flexible server at facility 1 and $c_2 = 2$ specialized servers at facility 2. Furthermore, the routing policy of Equation (3.3) with $\omega = 0.5$ is applied. All possible transitions between states and the corresponding transition rates for this case are given in the state transition diagram in Figure 3.2.

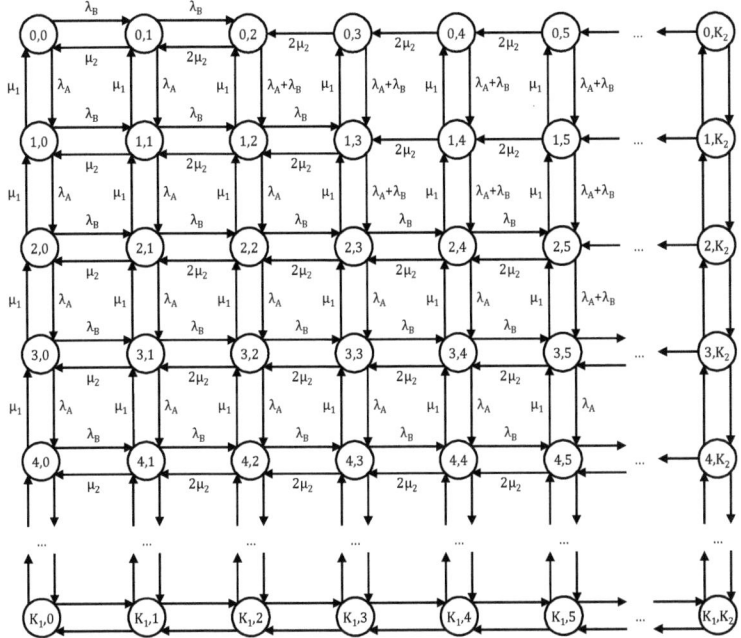

Figure 3.2: State transition diagram for the considered real-world case

3.4 Approximation of time-dependent performance measures

3.4.1 The stationary independent period-by-period approach

The main idea of the stationary independent period-by-period (SIPP) approximation is that a queueing system's performance in a period can be replaced by its steady-state values (Green et al. (2001)). The periods are analyzed independently. Time horizon T is divided into periods $[a_i, b_i]$ ($i \in I$) of same length l to apply the SIPP approximation to the truck handling system described in Section 3.2. The input arrival rates $\lambda_A(i)$

and $\lambda_B(i)$ for period i are time-averages, i.e.,

$$\lambda_A(i) = \frac{1}{l} \cdot \int\limits_{t=a_i}^{b_i} \lambda_A(t)\,dt \quad \text{and} \quad \lambda_B(i) = \frac{1}{l} \cdot \int\limits_{t=a_i}^{b_i} \lambda_B(t)\,dt. \quad (3.17)$$

The steady-state model of Section 3.3 is solved for each period i and the performance of the whole period is set to be equal to the derived steady-state performance.

3.4.2 The stationary backlog-carryover approach

Introduced by Stolletz (2008a) for homogeneous systems, the stationary backlog-carryover (SBC) approach uses steady-state solutions in a similar way to the SIPP approach. However, unlike the SIPP approach, the SBC approach connects succeeding periods with each other. Thus, the SBC approach builds backlogs of non-served arrivals in a period that are carried over to the succeeding period.

Similar to the SIPP approach, time horizon T is divided into periods i with constant parameters. Two evaluation steps are performed for every period i. In the first step, the corresponding *stationary loss system* is considered and the expected utilization as well as the expected probability of blocking are determined. These calculations make use of an artificial arrival rate that includes the actual arrival rate and a backlog carried over from the previous period. The backlog of a period is derived based on the artificial arrival rate and the resulting expected probability of blocking in the same period. In the second step of the SBC approach, the performance of the original system is approximated by a *stationary waiting system*. A modified arrival rate is used as an input for these calculations. This modified arrival rate is chosen so that the expected utilization of the considered waiting system equals the expected utilization of the loss queueing system from the first step of the SBC.

The basic idea of the SBC approach can also be used to analyze heterogeneous queueing systems. Thereby, the two steps of the basic SBC approximation are performed for every period i by applying the modifications described in the remainder of this section.

In the first step, the corresponding loss system is considered and the expected utilizations of both facilities, $E[U_1^{(loss)}(i)]$ and $E[U_2^{(loss)}(i)]$, as well as the expected blocking probabilities for arriving jobs of both truck classes, $E[P_A^{block(loss)}(i)]$ and $E[P_B^{block(loss)}(i)]$, are determined. These calculations are made by using the steady-state model from Section 3.3 with $K_1 = c_1$ and $K_2 = c_2$. Thereby, artificial arrival rates $\tilde{\lambda}_A(i)$ and $\tilde{\lambda}_B(i)$ for both truck classes are used as inputs. In accordance with the standard version of the SBC approach, these artificial arrival rates include the actual arrival rates and possible backlogs, $b_A(i-1)$ and $b_B(i-1)$, which are carried over from the preceding period (Eq. (3.18) and (3.19)).

$$\tilde{\lambda}_A(i) = \lambda_A(i) + b_A(i-1)$$
$$= \lambda_A(i) + \tilde{\lambda}_A(i-1) \cdot E[P_A^{block(loss)}(i-1)] \quad (3.18)$$
$$\tilde{\lambda}_B(i) = \lambda_B(i) + b_B(i-1)$$
$$= \lambda_B(i) + \tilde{\lambda}_B(i-1) \cdot E[P_B^{block(loss)}(i-1)] \quad (3.19)$$

In the second step, the performance of the original system is approximated by the performance of the corresponding waiting system. The maximum values for capacities K_1 and K_2 of both handling facilities have to be chosen so that the unlimited waiting system is sufficiently approximated by a loss-waiting system. The quality of the approximation can be measured by the blocking probabilities for both truck classes, which are reduced with increasing values of K_1 and K_2. Modified truck arrival rates λ_1^{MAR} and λ_2^{MAR} at both handling facilities are determined to calculate the performance of the waiting system. This determination is performed in a way such that the utilization of a handling facility in the considered waiting system equals the respective utilization of the corresponding loss system, i.e.,

$$\lambda_1^{MAR}(i) = c_1 \cdot \mu_1 \cdot \mathrm{E}[U_1^{(loss)}(i)] \tag{3.20}$$

and

$$\lambda_2^{MAR}(i) = c_2 \cdot \mu_2 \cdot \mathrm{E}[U_2^{(loss)}(i)]. \tag{3.21}$$

However, the truck class-dependent modified arrival rates $\lambda_A^{MAR}(i)$ and $\lambda_B^{MAR}(i)$ are required for the determination of the steady-state probabilities. These arrival rates are calculated based on the modified arrival rates for each facility and in such a way that the ratio of the modified arrival rates for each truck class $\lambda_A^{MAR}(i)$ and $\lambda_B^{MAR}(i)$ equals the ratio of the corresponding actual arrival rates $\lambda_A(i)$ and $\lambda_B(i)$, i.e., Equation (3.22) must hold.

$$\frac{\lambda_A^{MAR}(i)}{\lambda_B^{MAR}(i)} = \frac{\lambda_A(i)}{\lambda_B(i)} \tag{3.22}$$

Furthermore, the sum of the modified arrival rates at both facilities must be identical to the sum of the modified arrival rates of both truck classes (Eq. (3.23)).

$$\lambda_A^{MAR}(i) + \lambda_B^{MAR}(i) = \lambda_1^{MAR}(i) + \lambda_2^{MAR}(i) \tag{3.23}$$

The transformation of Equations (3.22) and (3.23) results in the modified arrival rates $\lambda_A^{MAR}(i)$ and $\lambda_B^{MAR}(i)$ for each truck class, i.e.,

$$\lambda_A^{MAR}(i) = \frac{\lambda_A(i)}{\lambda_A(i) + \lambda_B(i)} \cdot \left(\lambda_1^{MAR}(i) + \lambda_2^{MAR}(i)\right) \tag{3.24}$$

and

$$\lambda_B^{MAR}(i) = \frac{\lambda_B(i)}{\lambda_A(i) + \lambda_B(i)} \cdot \left(\lambda_1^{MAR}(i) + \lambda_2^{MAR}(i)\right). \tag{3.25}$$

Subsequently, these modified arrival rates are used to determine the steady-state probabilities of the truck handling system by applying the steady-state model, as described in Section 3.3. The performance measures of period i are approximated with the respective steady-state values. The complete pseudo code for the application of the SBC approach is given in Algorithm 3.1.

Algorithm 3.1 SBC for the truck handling system

1: Input: $\lambda_A(i)$, $\lambda_B(i)$, μ_1, μ_2, c_1, c_2, K_1, K_2, I
2: Initialization: $b_A(0) = 0$, $b_B(0) = 0$
3: **for** $i := 1$ **to** I **do**
4:     $\tilde{\lambda}_A(i) = \lambda_A(i) + b_A(i-1)$
5:     $\tilde{\lambda}_B(i) = \lambda_B(i) + b_B(i-1)$
6:     **procedure** LOSS SYSTEM($\tilde{\lambda}_A(i)$, $\tilde{\lambda}_B(i)$, μ_1, μ_2, c_1, c_2, $R(n_1, n_2)$)
7:         **return** $\mathrm{E}[P_A^{block\,(loss)}(i)]$, $\mathrm{E}[P_B^{block\,(loss)}(i)]$, $\mathrm{E}[U_1^{(loss)}(i)]$, $\mathrm{E}[U_2^{(loss)}(i)]$
8:     **end procedure**
9:     $b_A(i) = \tilde{\lambda}_A(i) \cdot \mathrm{E}[P_A^{block\,(loss)}(i)]$
10:    $b_B(i) = \tilde{\lambda}_B(i) \cdot \mathrm{E}[P_B^{block\,(loss)}(i)]$
11:    $\lambda_1^{MAR}(i) = c_1 \cdot \mu_1 \cdot \mathrm{E}[U_1^{(loss)}(i)]$
12:    $\lambda_2^{MAR}(i) = c_2 \cdot \mu_2 \cdot \mathrm{E}[U_2^{(loss)}(i)]$
13:    $\lambda_A^{MAR}(i) = \frac{\lambda_A(i)}{\lambda_A(i)+\lambda_B(i)} \cdot \left(\lambda_1^{MAR}(i) + \lambda_2^{MAR}(i)\right)$
14:    $\lambda_B^{MAR}(i) = \frac{\lambda_B(i)}{\lambda_A(i)+\lambda_B(i)} \cdot \left(\lambda_1^{MAR}(i) + \lambda_2^{MAR}(i)\right)$
15:    **procedure** LOSS-WAITING SYSTEM($\lambda_A^{MAR}(i)$, $\lambda_B^{MAR}(i)$, μ_1, μ_2, c_1, c_2, K_1, K_2, $R(n_1, n_2)$)
16:        **return** Time-dependent performance measures
17:    **end procedure**
18: **end for**

3.5 Numerical study

3.5.1 Steady-state performance analysis

The first part of our numerical study analyzes the impact of the truncation of the state space in the steady-state model. Furthermore, we analyze the long-term behavior of the SBC approach using constant rates and then compare our results to theoretical steady-state values. The subsequent analysis is based on the original truck handling system with $c_1 = 1$ server at facility 1, with $c_2 = 2$ servers at facility 2, and with the routing policy delineated in Equation (3.3) with $\omega = 0.5$. Four different combinations of arrival rates are considered ($\lambda_A \in \{0.7, 0.9\}$, $\lambda_B \in \{1.4, 1.8\}$), all of which result in different loads $\rho = (\lambda_A + \lambda_B)/(c_1 \cdot \mu_1 + c_2 \cdot \mu_2)$. The processing rate at each facility is set to $\mu_1 = \mu_2 = 1$.

The impact of the state space truncation via finite $K = K_1 = K_2$ on the expected number of trucks at each facility is illustrated in Tables 3.1 and 3.2. These tables compare the results of the steady-state model from Section 3.3 with a limited K to the simulation results with an unlimited state space, i.e., $K = \infty$. The last column of each table includes the 95% confidence intervals of the simulation results for 1,000,000 replications considering one time unit after a warm-up phase of 2,000 time units. These confidence intervals are supposed to be small enough so that the simulation results can be used as benchmark for the steady-state values. The approximation quality of the steady-state model increases with a larger state space for all considered arrival rate combinations. This result can be explained by decreasing blocking probabilities for increasing truncation limits K. The dependencies of the expected blocking probabilities $\mathrm{E}[P_A^{block}]$ and $\mathrm{E}[P_B^{block}]$ on K are shown in Table 3.3. In the considered cases, the steady-state performance values are well approximated by the steady-state model when the system parameters $K = K_1 = K_2$ are chosen to be larger or equal to 50 trucks. In these cases, the maximum expected blocking probabilities are considerably small with $\mathrm{E}[P_A^{block}] = 7.57 \cdot 10^{-4}$ for trucks of class A and $\mathrm{E}[P_B^{block}] = 4.76 \cdot 10^{-5}$ for trucks of class B. Moreover, the relative deviation of the expected number of trucks at each facility does not exceed 3.00%. However, dependent on the data, the truncation limits have to be adjusted.

Table 3.1: Steady-state values of $E[L_1^S]$ and the relative deviations from the simulation results

Input	$K = 25$	$K = 50$	$K = 75$	$K = 100$	Simulation ($K = \infty$)
$\lambda_A = 0.7, \lambda_B = 1.4$ ($\rho = 0.7$)	3.0689 (-0.16%)	3.0723 (-0.05%)	3.0723 (-0.05%)	3.0723 (-0.05%)	3.0739 [$\pm$0.0058]
$\lambda_A = 0.9, \lambda_B = 1.4$ ($\rho = 0.77$)	8.0015 (-19.55%)	9.6891 (-2.58%)	9.9217 (-0.25%)	9.9470 (0.01%)	9.9462 [$\pm$0.0188]
$\lambda_A = 0.7, \lambda_B = 1.8$ ($\rho = 0.83$)	4.0907 (-0.46%)	4.1136 (0.09%)	4.1136 (0.09%)	4.1136 (0.09%)	4.1097 [$\pm$0.0066]
$\lambda_A = 0.9, \lambda_B = 1.8$ ($\rho = 0.9$)	9.3829 (-21.94%)	11.6586 (-3.00%)	11.9665 (-0.44%)	11.9994 (-0.17%)	12.0195 [$\pm$0.0196]

Table 3.2: Steady-state values of $E[L_2^S]$ and the relative deviations from the simulation results

Input	$K = 25$	$K = 50$	$K = 75$	$K = 100$	Simulation ($K = \infty$)
$\lambda_A = 0.7, \lambda_B = 1.4$ ($\rho = 0.7$)	1.9237 (-0.15%)	1.9238 (-0.15%)	1.9238 (-0.15%)	1.9238 (-0.15%)	1.9266 [$\pm$0.0035]
$\lambda_A = 0.9, \lambda_B = 1.4$ ($\rho = 0.77$)	2.3712 (-1.16%)	2.3969 (-0.08%)	2.3986 (-0.01%)	2.3987 (-0.01%)	2.3989 [$\pm$0.0046]
$\lambda_A = 0.7, \lambda_B = 1.8$ ($\rho = 0.83$)	3.7898 (-0.67%)	3.8183 (0.08%)	3.8184 (0.08%)	3.8184 (0.08%)	3.8154 [$\pm$0.0071]
$\lambda_A = 0.9, \lambda_B = 1.8$ ($\rho = 0.9$)	5.6911 (-10.47%)	6.3076 (-0.77%)	6.3445 (-0.19%)	6.3465 (-0.16%)	6.3568 [$\pm$0.0124]

Table 3.3: Steady-state values of $E[P_A^{block}]$ and $E[P_B^{block}]$

Input		$K = 25$	$K = 50$	$K = 75$	$K = 100$
$\lambda_A = 0.7, \lambda_B = 1.4$ ($\rho = 0.7$)	$E[P_A^{block}]$	$5.73 \cdot 10^{-5}$	$7.69 \cdot 10^{-9}$	$1.03 \cdot 10^{-12}$	$1.38 \cdot 10^{-16}$
	$E[P_B^{block}]$	$6.44 \cdot 10^{-7}$	$1.08 \cdot 10^{-12}$	$1.56 \cdot 10^{-18}$	$2.59 \cdot 10^{-24}$
$\lambda_A = 0.9, \lambda_B = 1.4$ ($\rho = 0.77$)	$E[P_A^{block}]$	$8.63 \cdot 10^{-3}$	$5.78 \cdot 10^{-4}$	$4.13 \cdot 10^{-5}$	$2.97 \cdot 10^{-6}$
	$E[P_B^{block}]$	$1.00 \cdot 10^{-5}$	$4.30 \cdot 10^{-10}$	$1.59 \cdot 10^{-14}$	$5.88 \cdot 10^{-19}$
$\lambda_A = 0.7, \lambda_B = 1.8$ ($\rho = 0.83$)	$E[P_A^{block}]$	$1.01 \cdot 10^{-4}$	$1.56 \cdot 10^{-8}$	$2.12 \cdot 10^{-12}$	$2.85 \cdot 10^{-16}$
	$E[P_B^{block}]$	$2.35 \cdot 10^{-4}$	$2.67 \cdot 10^{-7}$	$2.75 \cdot 10^{-10}$	$3.08 \cdot 10^{-13}$
$\lambda_A = 0.9, \lambda_B = 1.8$ ($\rho = 0.9$)	$E[P_A^{block}]$	$1.04 \cdot 10^{-2}$	$7.57 \cdot 10^{-4}$	$5.46 \cdot 10^{-5}$	$3.92 \cdot 10^{-6}$
	$E[P_B^{block}]$	$2.16 \cdot 10^{-3}$	$4.76 \cdot 10^{-5}$	$9.47 \cdot 10^{-7}$	$1.87 \cdot 10^{-8}$

In a second set of experiments, we run the SBC approach with constant arrival rates by applying the four arrival rate combinations described above. After a certain period $\bar{i}$, all parameters and performance measures no longer change from one period to the succeeding period. All resulting performance measures converge to the respective measurements from the steady-state model of Section 3.3. The numerical results demonstrate that the SBC approach reaches the steady-state in the considered cases.

3.5.2 Time-dependent performance analysis

The following numerical experiments analyze the SBC approach's capability to describe the system's transient and time-dependent behavior. Therefore, the SBC approach is compared to the estimates obtained from simulation and to the results of the SIPP approximation. The SIPP approach is chosen because this method is frequently used to analyze the time-dependent behavior of a system under non-stationary conditions (Green et al. (2001)) and because this approach provides comparatively good approximation results (Ingolfsson et al. (2007)).

In accordance with the truck handling operations described in Section 3.1, the system configuration for our analysis is characterized by $c_1 = 1$ and $c_2 = 2$ servers and the routing policy delineated in Equation (3.3) with $\omega = 0.5$. The service rates are assumed to be constant at $\mu_1 = \mu_2 = 1$. Table 3.4 illustrates piecewise constant arrival rates $\lambda_A(t)$ and $\lambda_B(t)$ over a time horizon of 1000 time units and the corresponding system load in terms of $\rho(t) = (\lambda_A(t) + \lambda_B(t))/(c_1 \cdot \mu_1 + c_2 \cdot \mu_2)$. This artificial dataset incorporates shocks in terms of increasing and decreasing arrival rates, accounts for asymmetric developments of $\lambda_A(t)$ and $\lambda_B(t)$, and includes a period of temporary overload in $t = [400; 450)$. With the exception of this overload period, the arrival rates are chosen such that the system is able to reach a steady state for each arrival rate combination. According to the preliminary results of the steady-state analysis, the system parameters K_1 and K_2 are chosen to be 50 for the SIPP and SBC approximations.

As recommended by Stolletz (2008a), a period length of $l = \mu^{-1} = 1$ is applied in the SBC approach. For the SIPP approach, a period length of $l = 50$ is chosen as the arrival rates remain constant for at least 50 periods and, therefore, the application of a shorter period length is not beneficial.

Table 3.4: Input arrival rates for time-dependent performance evaluation

t	[0;100)	[100;200)	[200;400)	[400;450)	[450;700)	[700;900)	[900;1000)
$\lambda_A(t)$	0.2	0.6	0.6	0.8	0.6	0.6	0.2
$\lambda_B(t)$	1.2	1.2	1.8	2.3	2.0	1.6	1.0
$\rho(t)$	0.47	0.6	0.8	1.03	0.87	0.73	0.4

Figures 3.3 and 3.4 show the time-dependent expected number of trucks at each facility, $E[L_1^S(t)]$ and $E[L_2^S(t)]$, as well as the expected waiting times per truck at each facility, $E[W_1^Q(t)]$ and $E[W_2^Q(t)]$. The SIPP approach calculates merely steady-state values and, thus, ignores the transient behavior of the system's performance. The development of the performance measures is therefore characterized by a stepwise trajectory. Because of the limitation of the system size by parameters K_1 and K_2, a steady state is achieved even in the case of overload for periods $t = [400; 450)$. However, this results in a significant overestimation of the actual values in these periods as no transient phases are taken into account. In contrast, the SBC approach considers the transient behavior and therefore comes significantly closer to the simulation results than the SIPP approximation for these periods. Both the expected time-dependent numbers of trucks at each facility, $E[L_1^S(t)]$ and $E[L_2^S(t)]$, and the expected waiting times per truck, $E[W_1^Q(t)]$ and $E[W_2^Q(t)]$, are well approximated by the SBC approach.

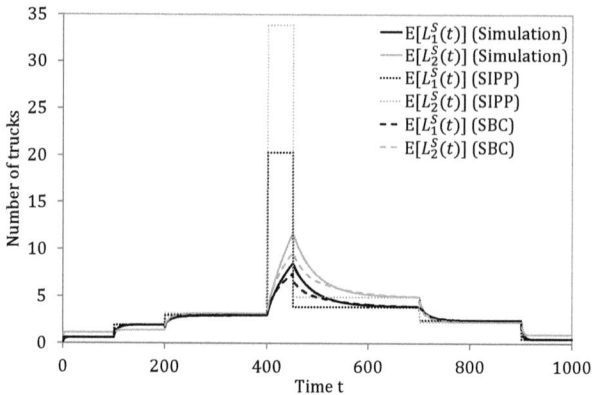

Figure 3.3: Time-dependent expected number of trucks at each handling facility

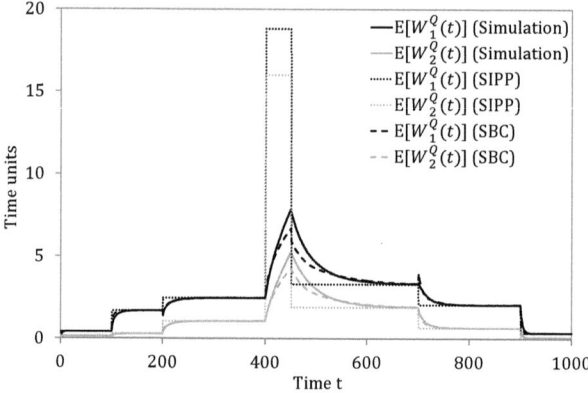

Figure 3.4: Time-dependent expected waiting time of a truck at each handling facility

Figure 3.5 shows the expected time-dependent utilization of each handling facility, $E[U_1(t)]$ and $E[U_2(t)]$, which reveals that the SIPP approach reaches the correct steady-state values for each facility in underloaded periods. Once again, the SBC approach approximates time-dependent behavior better than the SIPP approach because the SBC approach also traces the transient phases of the system's behavior.

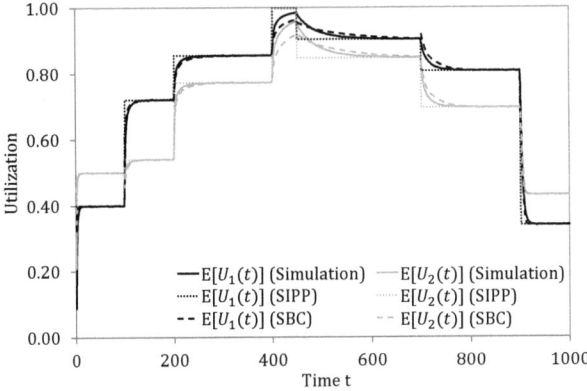

Figure 3.5: Time-dependent expected utilization of each handling facility

Figures 3.3 to 3.5 reveal that both, the SIPP and SBC approaches, properly predict steady-state values. The SBC approach also achieves good approximation results for transient phases. Therefore, it obviously outperforms the SIPP approximation by providing reliable expected values of time-dependent performance measures. The SBC approach achieves a high approximation quality for a wide range of the overall system utilization without depending on the arrival rate configuration.

3.5.3 Performance analysis of non-stationary real-world data

This section analyzes the real-word air cargo terminal with $c_1 = 1$ and $c_2 = 2$ servers and with the routing policy delineated in Equation (3.3) with $\omega = 0.5$. Figure 3.6 illustrates an excerpt of the typical arrival patterns and the corresponding system load $\rho(t)$ from a Wednesday at 12:00 am to a Friday at 12:00 am. The data shows that the arrival rate of class B per hour $\lambda_B(t)$ considerably exceeds the arrival rate of class A per hour $\lambda_A(t)$. The system load reaches its maximum of 0.998 on Thursday morning between 1:00 am and 2:00 am.

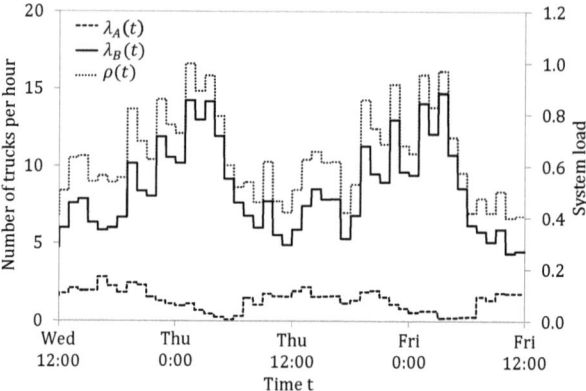

Figure 3.6: Real-world data on time-dependent arrival rates and system load

Service times differ between the facilities as a result of different conveyor processes. The distribution of the handling times at facility 1 is shown in Figure 3.7. The mean service time is 8.93 minutes per truck (i.e., $\mu_1 = 6.72$ trucks per hour) and the coefficient of variation is 1.10. Trucks at facility 2 are processed in 13.87 minutes per truck on average (i.e., $\mu_2 = 4.33$ trucks per hour) with a coefficient of variation of 1.13, see the distribution in Figure 3.8. The distributions are not exponential, but the comparison of simulation results of the number of trucks in the overall system and at facility 1 based on empirical, exponentially distributed, and deterministic service times reveals that such an assumption is reasonable, see Figure 3.9. Neglecting stochasticity at all leads to a significant underestimation of the expected number of trucks in the system.

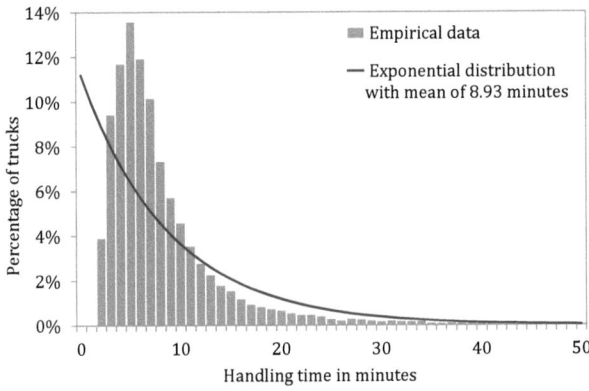

Figure 3.7: Empirical distribution and exponential approximation of handling times at facility 1

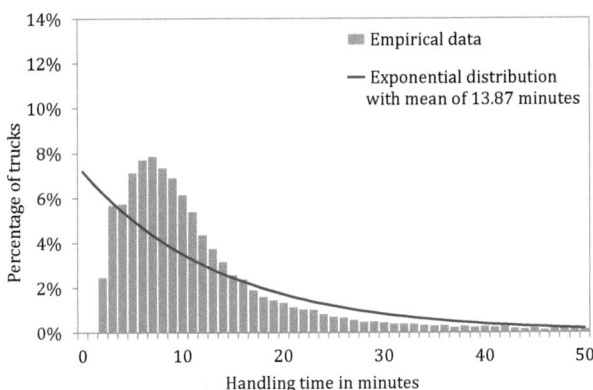

Figure 3.8: Empirical distribution and exponential approximation of handling times at facility 2

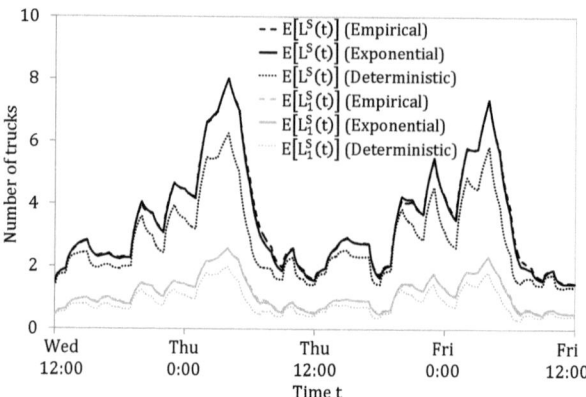

Figure 3.9: Comparison of the simulation results of the number of trucks in the overall system and at facility 1 based on empirical handling times and the exponential and deterministic approximations

The performance evaluation is again conducted through the SIPP approach, the SBC approach, and by simulation. Empirical performance data are not available for the analyzed air cargo system. Collecting such data would require a long observation period with a stable arrival pattern to reach the same confidence intervals as by simulation. Furthermore, the comparison to simulation allows a direct judgment of the reliability of the approaches as deviations in the performance measures are not due to additional external effects in the observed data.

The weighted average service time of all servers is $(c_1 \cdot \mu_1 + c_2 \cdot \mu_2)/(c_1 + c_2) = 12.22$ minutes per truck. Therefore, a period length of $l = 12$ minutes is chosen for the SBC and the SIPP approach. Based on the results of Section 3.5.1, system parameters K_1 and K_2 are again chosen to be 50 for the SIPP and SBC approximations. This results in sufficiently small maximum instantaneous blocking probabilities of $\mathrm{E}\left[P_A^{block}\right] = 6.11 \cdot 10^{-20}$ for trucks of class A and $\mathrm{E}\left[P_B^{block}\right] = 9.03 \cdot 10^{-6}$ for trucks of class B.

Figure 3.10 shows the expected time-dependent behavior of the number of trucks at facility 1 ($\mathrm{E}[L_1^S(t)]$). The SIPP approximation significantly overestimates in periods close to critical load and underestimates in the following periods with underload because this approach does not consider any carryovers from previous periods. The SBC approach, however, comes quite close to determining the expected performance from simulation for each period. Figure 3.11 shows similar results for the expected time-dependent waiting time per truck at handling facility 2 ($E[W_2^Q(t)]$).

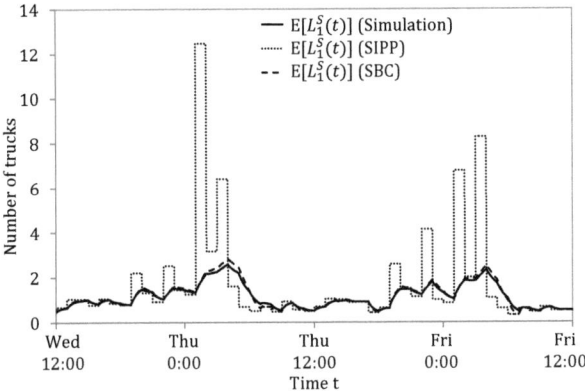

Figure 3.10: Expected time-dependent number of trucks at handling facility 1

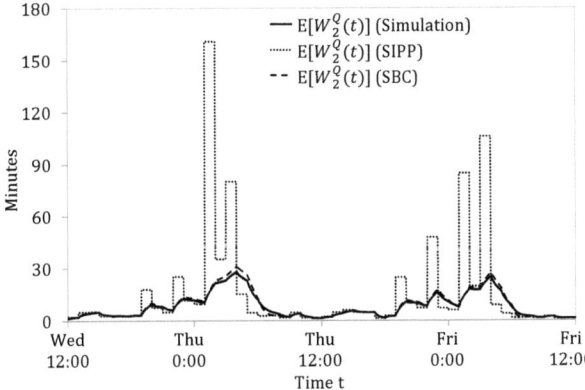

Figure 3.11: Expected time-dependent waiting time per truck at handling facility 2

3.5.4 Sensitivity Analysis

To derive further managerial insights from the application of the SBC approximation, we conduct a sensitivity analysis with respect to server capacities (Analysis I), demand (Analysis II), and routing policies (Analysis III). This performance evaluation is based on the same system configuration, input rates, and method parameters as in the previous base case analysis.

Analysis I assesses the impact of a second flexible server at handling facility 1 ($c_1 = 2$). Due to this increased capacity, the routing decision delineated in Equation (3.3) is adjusted with $\omega = 1.0$ in order to achieve some kind of balanced loads between both facilities. We assume the service rates per server to be independent of the number of severs at a particular facility. This is a reasonable assumption as there is no obvious interference in parallel handling processes. However, our model could be easily adapted to account for a proportional deduction in the overall process rate by introducing a corresponding parameter. The time-dependent expected values of the average waiting time per truck for the overall system ($\mathrm{E}[W^Q(t)]$) as well as for the utilizations at facilities 1 and 2 ($\mathrm{E}[U_1(t)]$, $\mathrm{E}[U_2(t)]$) are presented in Figures 3.12 to 3.14, respectively, also providing the performance of the base case scenario for the purpose of comparison. Figure 3.12 reveals that a second truck dock at facility 1 could significantly reduce waiting times. However, this additional server would lead to a lower and, therefore, less efficient utilization of handling facility 1 (see Figure 3.13). Figure 3.14 similarly shows a reduction of the utilization of handling facility 2. This reduction can be explained by additional routings to facility 1. Because of the increased parameter ω, the routing decision $R_\omega(n_1, n_2)$ changes in a way that increases the number of states with possible routing to handling facility 1. The set of states

$$\mathcal{S}' = \left\{ (n_1, n_2) \mid n_2 \geq c_2 \wedge 0.5 \leq \frac{n_1}{n_2} < 1 \right\} \tag{3.26}$$

describes the corresponding additional system states in which an arriving truck of class B is routed to facility 1 in contrast to the base case of $c_1 = 1$. Therefore, the utilization of facility 1 within Analysis I is higher than only half of the utilization in the base case.

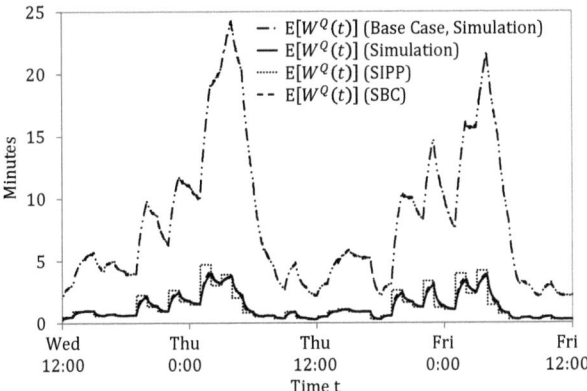

Figure 3.12: Expected time-dependent average waiting time per truck for the overall system after opening a second server at handling facility 1 (Analysis I)

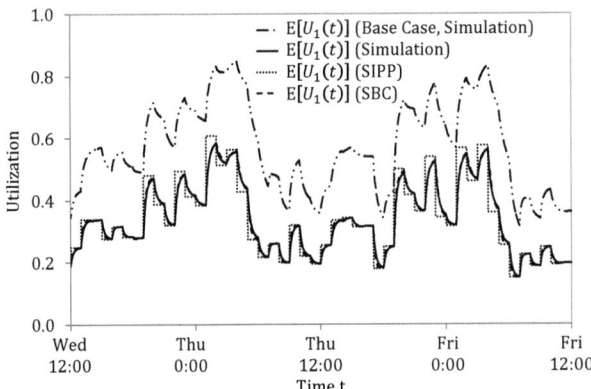

Figure 3.13: Expected time-dependent utilization at handling facility 1 after opening a second server at handling facility 1 (Analysis I)

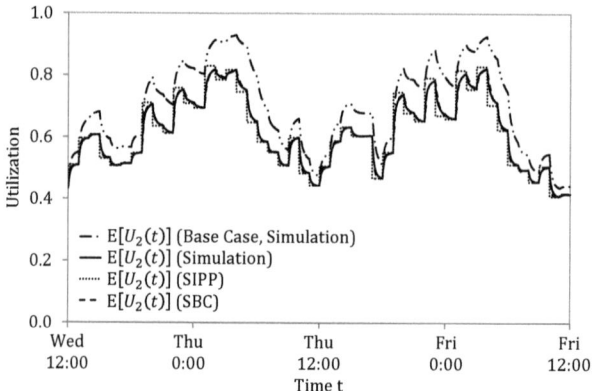

Figure 3.14: Expected time-dependent utilization at handling facility 2 after opening a second server at handling facility 1 (Analysis I)

Analysis II evaluates the impact of an increase in demand by 10% for each time interval. The number of servers at handling facility 1 is reset to the initial situation of $c_1 = 1$. While in the base scenario, temporary overload has not been existent, the increased demand results in system loads $\rho(t) \geq 1$ on Thursday 1:00 - 2:00 am, 3:00 - 4:00 am, and 10:00 - 11:00 pm and on Friday 1:00 - 2:00 am, and 3:00 - 4:00 am. A comparison of the corresponding expected time-dependent average waiting time per truck for the overall system ($\mathrm{E}[W^Q(t)]$) to the base case scenario is provided in Figure 3.15. The graph shows that the demand increase by 10% results in increasing waiting times. The maximum waiting time increases by 55.2% from 24.24 to 37.61 minutes per truck.

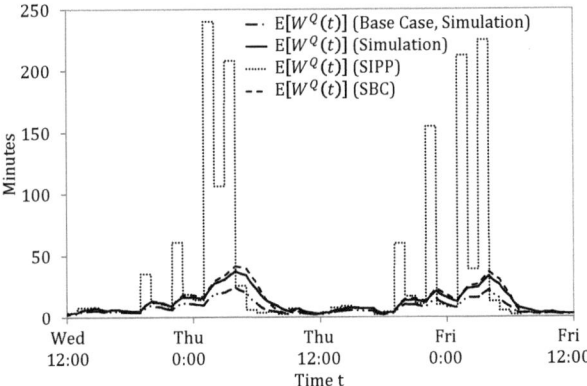

Figure 3.15: Expected time-dependent average waiting time per truck for the overall system after an 10%-increase in demand (Analysis II)

Analysis III assesses the impact of the state-dependent routing policy on the number of trucks in the system. To generalize the routing policy $R_\omega(n_1, n_2)$ from Equation (3.3), let ϑ be a threshold on the number of trucks at facility 2. The resulting routing decision is defined by

$$R_{\vartheta,\omega}(n_1, n_2) = \begin{cases} 1, & \text{if} \quad n_2 \geq \vartheta \quad \wedge \quad n_1 < \omega \cdot n_2, \\ 0, & \text{otherwise.} \end{cases} \tag{3.27}$$

For $\vartheta = 2$ and $\omega = 0.5$, policy $R_{\vartheta,\omega}(n_1, n_2)$ equals to the original one assumed in Subsection 3.5.3. The number of states allowing for routing increases with decreasing ϑ and increasing ω. Table 3.5 shows the time-averaged probability $\overline{\mathrm{E}[P_B^{route}]}$ that an arriving truck of class B is allocated to facility 1 and the time-averaged expected number of trucks in the system $\overline{\mathrm{E}[L^S]}$. Routing policies $R_{\vartheta,\omega}(n_1, n_2)$ are applied with all combinations of $\vartheta \in \{1, ..., 6\}$ and $\omega \in \{0.25, 0.5, 0.75, 1.0, 1.25\}$.

Table 3.5: Time-averaged routing probability and time-averaged expected number of trucks in the system ($\mathrm{E}[P_B^{route}]$ / $\mathrm{E}[L^S]$) dependent on the thresholds ϑ and ω

ϑ	$\omega = 0.25$	$\omega = 0.5$	$\omega = 0.75$	$\omega = 1.0$	$\omega = 1.25$
1	32.87% / 3.47	34.92% / 3.28	37.75% / 3.29	37.90% / 3.30	43.40% / 3.57
2	25.14% / 3.53	27.13% / 3.33	30.47% / 3.34	30.65% / 3.35	32.49% / 3.48
3	20.50% / 3.72	22.89% / 3.51	24.14% / 3.50	24.38% / 3.51	25.10% / 3.57
4	17.70% / 3.97	18.97% / 3.78	19.66% / 3.75	20.06% / 3.76	20.41% / 3.79
5	16.05% / 4.22	16.61% / 4.09	16.95% / 4.07	17.12% / 4.07	17.35% / 4.09
6	14.28% / 4.57	14.69% / 4.44	14.97% / 4.40	15.04% / 4.40	15.18% / 4.41

As expected, the average routing probability $\overline{\mathrm{E}[P_B^{route}]}$ decreases with increasing ϑ and increases in ω. The average number of trucks in the system increases in ϑ for all values of ω with the exception of $\omega = 1.25$. In this case the average number of trucks in the system reaches a minimum at $\vartheta = 2$. With respect to $\overline{\mathrm{E}[L^S]}$, the policy is relatively insensitive to changes in ω. The lowest average number of trucks over all analyzed policies is observed for $\vartheta = 1$ and $\omega = 0.5$. Under this policy, 34.92% of trucks of class B are routed to the flexible server.

3.6 Conclusion

In this paper, we developed an accurate approximation approach for the time-dependent performance analysis of truck handling operations at an air cargo terminal. The underlying system features heterogeneous classes of trucks, heterogeneous classes of servers at two parallel handling facilities, and the routing of trucks upon arrival. We provide a general model for multiple parallel servers and for arbitrary system-dependent routing policies. By formulating a Markov chain and the corresponding system of equations, we derived the steady-state performance measures. We then developed an SBC approach for approximating the time-dependent performance of the considered heterogeneous queueing system. The numerical study shows that the SBC approach outperforms the SIPP approach in the evaluation of the system's transient and time-dependent behavior. This observation also holds for periods of overload. Our analysis was based on artificial and on real-world input data, indicating the applicability of our approach.

With respect to further research, the extension of the SBC approximation so that it integrates time-dependent truncation limits could be useful in order to improve the accuracy of the performance approximation. Furthermore, future research could integrate the developed performance approximation into a decision model. For example, the optimization of the routing policy, the provision of decision support for time-dependent capacity supply, or an active management of truck arrivals by means of stochastic appointment scheduling approaches would be notable topics for further research.

4 Time-dependent performance analysis of queueing systems with generally distributed abandonments

Co-authors:

Raik Stolletz
Chair of Production Management, Business School, University of Mannheim, Germany

Thomas I. Maindl
Department of Astrophysics, University of Vienna, Austria

Published as:

Working paper

Abstract:

In many service systems, such as call centers, customers leave the queue if their waiting time exceeds their personal patience. These abandonments typically follow a general distribution. Furthermore, such queueing systems are characterized by time-dependent arrival processes.

This paper develops a new stationary backlog-carryover (SBC) approximation for the performance evaluation of non-stationary $M(t)/M/c + G$ queueing systems with a continuous adjustment of the underlying interval length. For stationary parameters, we show that if the approach converges, it converges to the $M/M/c + G$ queueing system. For time-dependent arrival rates, a numerical study compares the new approach, the modified offered load (MOL) approximation, and the traditional stationary independent period-by-period (SIPP) approach. For exponentially distributed patience times, the numerical solution of the Chapman-Kolmogorov equations is used as benchmark. For generally distributed abandonments, the approaches are compared to simulation. Additionally, we apply the new approach to the performance evaluation of a real-world call center.

4.1 Introduction

In many service systems, customers leave the queue before being served due to their personal impatience. For example in call centers, customers are willing to wait until their maximum accepted waiting time is reached and then decide to hang up (see, e.g., Koole and Mandelbaum (2002)). The distribution of the maximum accepted waiting time is often assumed to follow an exponential distribution. However, several studies claim that this assumption may be crucial and the consideration of generally distributed abandonment times is necessary (see, e.g., Mandelbaum and Zeltyn (2004)). Furthermore, such queueing systems are often characterized by non-stationary behavior due to nonhomogeneous arrival processes (see, e.g., Brown et al. (2005)). Such a call center described above can be modeled as an $M(t)/M/c + G$ queueing system that includes a time-dependent arrival process and generally distributed abandonments. There still exist approaches for the analysis of such queueing systems with stationary parameters ignoring any time-dependency. Thus, we base our performance analysis on approaches that use stationary models in the analysis of time-dependent systems.

This paper deals with algorithms that enable the performance evaluation of an $M(t)/M/c + G$ queueing system with time-dependent arrival rate and abandonment times that follow any arbitrary distribution. We develop a stationary backlog-carryover (SBC) approach that allows for the analysis of such queueing systems. Additionally, we present an interval length adjustment that improves the accuracy of the SBC approach. The applicability of the SBC approximation to a wide range of system configurations is shown within a numerical study and its accuracy is compared to the modified offered load (MOL) approach. Furthermore, the new approach is applied to the example of a real-world call center.

The remainder of this paper is organized as follows. Section 4.2 presents the characteristics of the analyzed queueing model and gives an overview of the corresponding literature. Section 4.3 is dedicated to the description of the approaches for the time-dependent performance evaluation. It includes the solution of the Chapman-Kolmogorov equations (CKE) (Section 4.3.1), the SBC approximation (Section 4.3.2), and the MOL approach (Section 4.3.3). Section 4.4 outlines the behavior of the SBC approximation with stationary parameters. The performance of all approaches from Section 4.3 is analyzed in Section 4.5. It comprises the analysis of Markovian systems using artificial data (Section 4.5.1), the analysis of systems with generally distributed abandonments using artificial data (Section 4.5.2), and the analysis of a real-world call center (Section 4.5.3). Section 4.6 provides a conclusion and suggestions for further research.

4.2 System description and literature review

This section comprises the description of the analyzed queueing system (Section 4.2.1) and an overview of the corresponding literature (Section 4.2.2).

4.2.1 Queueing model description

We consider an $M(t)/M/c + G$ queueing system as depicted in Figure 4.1. Items arrive at the system according to a non-stationary Poisson process with time-dependent rate $\lambda(t)$. They are served by c parallel and identical servers with constant rate μ. If all servers are busy, arriving items have to wait in a waiting room with unlimited capacity. Waiting items are impatient and may leave the system before being served if the actual waiting time exceeds their patience. The maximum accepted waiting time of an item follows a general distribution that is given by the distribution function G with abandonment rate ν.

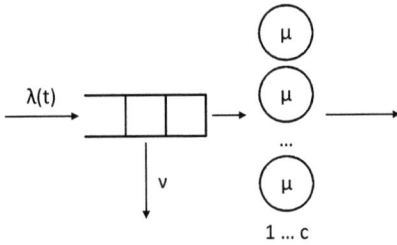

Figure 4.1: $M(t)/M/c + G$ queueing model description

4.2.2 Literature

The literature on methods for the performance evaluation of queueing systems with time-dependent input parameters is extensive and the different approaches can be classified into three groups according to the overview in Schwarz et al. (2016). These categories are (1) numerical and analytical solutions, (2) approaches based on models with piecewise constant parameters, and (3) approaches based on modified system characteristics. In the following, we concentrate on the work that incorporates the analysis of queueing systems with abandonments that can be either Markovian or non-Markovian.

The major part of the relevant literature deals with the analysis of Markovian queueing systems, i.e., systems with Poisson arrivals, exponentially distributed service times, and exponentially distributed abandonment times. Kim and Ha (2012) derive an explicit solution for the $M(t)/M/c(t) + M$ queueing system but restrict their analysis to systems in which the abandonment rate equals the service rate. Approaches that are based on models with piecewise constant parameters are used by Mok and Shanthikumar (1987), Steckley and Henderson (2007), Dietz (2011), and Creemers et al. (2014). Steckley and Henderson (2007) and Dietz (2011) focus on approaches that are based on stationary models and apply the pointwise stationary approach (PSA) and the stationary independent period-by-period (SIPP) approximation, respectively. Mok and

Shanthikumar (1987) use the uniformization/randomization technique in their analysis of $M(t)/M/c(t)/K + M$ queueing systems. The same approach is used by Creemers et al. (2014) for the analysis of $PH(t)/PH(t)/c(t) + PH(t)$ and $PH(t)/PH(t)/c(t) + PH(t)/K$ queueing systems. Further used approaches based on modified system characteristics include the fluid approximation (Mandelbaum et al. (2002), Aguir et al. (2004), Bertsimas and Doan (2010), Ko and Gautam (2013), Massey and Pender (2013), Pender (2014a)), the diffusion approximation (Mandelbaum et al. (2002), Ko and Gautam (2013), Massey and Pender (2013), Pender (2014a)), and the surrogate distribution approximation (Massey and Pender (2013), Pender (2014a), Pender (2014b)).

The analysis of non-Markovian queueing systems includes approaches based on models with piecewise constant parameters. Lackman et al. (1992) consider an $M(t)/D/1 + D$ queueing system with constant service and abandonment times in their analysis using a discrete time approach. A general idea for the modification of the MOL approach is given in Feldman et al. (2008) that allows for the analysis of $M(t)/G/c(t) + G$ queueing systems. However, the accuracy of the approximation has not been analyzed. An approach from the category of approaches based on modified system characteristics is used by Liu and Whitt (2011) and Liu and Whitt (2012b) for the analysis of more general queueing systems that include generally distributed abandonment times. Their fluid approximation ignores any stochasticity in the arrival, service, and abandonment times. Thus, their approach delivers good approximation results for systems in which the impact of stochasticity is negligible in comparison to the impact of time-dependency. This means that the accuracy of the approach increases with increasing number of parallel servers and that the approach is appropriate especially for systems in overload or underload.

In literature, there still exist approaches for the performance evaluation of stationary queueing systems with generally distributed abandonments. Thus, we focus on the SBC approximation and the MOL approach in our analysis of $M(t)/M/c + G$ queueing systems as both methods incorporate the use of stationary models as part of the performance evaluation. Even though both approaches are based on stationary models, they are assigned to different categories according to the classification scheme in Schwarz et al. (2016). Thus, approaches from all three categories are compared within this paper as the solution of the Chapman-Kolmogorov equations (CKE) is included for systems with Markovian abandonments.

4.3 Performance evaluation approaches

This section deals with three approaches for the performance evaluation of the considered queueing system. The derivation of the time-dependent performance based on the solution of the CKE is described in Section 4.3.1. Section 4.3.2 develops an SBC approximation and Section 4.3.3 describes the implemented MOL approach.

4.3.1 Solution of the Chapman-Kolmogorov equations

For $M(t)/M/c + M$ queueing systems, the CKE describe the time-dependent performance (see, e.g., Dietz (2011)). The current state n of the system at time t is given explicitly by the work in process $L^S(t)$, i.e., the number of items being processed on a server and the items waiting in the queue. The state transition diagram including the associated birth- and death rates is given in Figure 4.2.

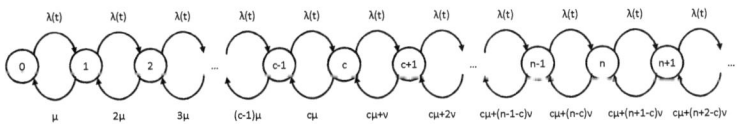

Figure 4.2: State transition diagram

Featuring an unlimited capacity, the $M(t)/M/c + M$ queueing system induces an infinite number of CKE. In order to make the system of CKE mathematically tractable, the infinite state space of the original system has to be truncated and a maximum number of considered states has to be chosen that equals the maximum considered number of customers in the system L_{max}^S. It has to be chosen sufficiently large such that the truncated system provides a good approximation of the original system. The system of CKE that describes the time-dependent behavior of this truncated system is given by Equations (4.1) to (4.4). Here, the vector $P(t) = (p_0(t), p_1(t), p_2(t), ..., p_{L_{max}^S}(t))$ consists of the state probabilities p_n at time t for all states $n \in \mathcal{S} = \{0, 1, 2, ..., L_{max}^S\}$.

$$\frac{dp_0(t)}{dt} = \mu \cdot p_1(t) - \lambda(t) \cdot p_0(t), \qquad \text{for } n = 0 \qquad (4.1)$$

$$\frac{dp_n(t)}{dt} = (n+1) \cdot \mu \cdot p_{n+1}(t) + \lambda(t) \cdot p_{n-1}(t)$$
$$- (\lambda(t) + n\mu) \cdot p_n(t), \qquad \text{for } 1 \leq n < c \quad (4.2)$$

$$\frac{dp_n(t)}{dt} = (c\mu + (n+1-c)\nu) \cdot p_{n+1}(t) + \lambda(t) \cdot p_{n-1}(t)$$
$$- (\lambda(t) + c\mu + (n-c)\nu) \cdot p_n(t), \quad \text{for } c \leq n < L_{max}^S$$
$$(4.3)$$

$$\frac{dp_n(t)}{dt} = \lambda(t) \cdot p_{n-1}(t)$$
$$- (c\mu + (n-c)\nu) \cdot p_n(t), \qquad \text{for } n = L_{max}^S \quad (4.4)$$

This system of ordinary differential equations describes the time evolution of the state probability vector $P(t)$. We directly solve it for time-dependent arrival rates $\lambda(t)$ by numerically integrating the CKE using the Dormand-Prince method (Dormand and Prince (1980)) which is an explicit embedded Runge-Kutta method with dense output and adaptive step size. It is using an error estimate based on comparing fifth-order to fourth-order accurate solutions and, thus, is of order 4(5).

The time-dependent state probabilities are then used to calculate the expected time-dependent number of waiting customers $E[L^Q(t)]$, the expected number of customers in the system $E[L^S(t)]$, and the expected time-dependent utilization of the system $E[U(t)]$ according to Equations (4.5) to (4.7).

$$E[L^Q(t)] = \sum_{n=c+1}^{L^S_{max}} (n - c) \cdot p_n(t) \qquad (4.5)$$

$$E[L^S(t)] = \sum_{n=0}^{L^S_{max}} n \cdot p_n(t) \qquad (4.6)$$

$$E[U(t)] = \sum_{n=0}^{L^S_{max}} \min\left\{\frac{n}{c}; 1\right\} \cdot p_n(t) \qquad (4.7)$$

4.3.2 The stationary backlog-carryover approach

The first part of this section includes a description of the SBC approximation for the performance evaluation of $M(t)/M/c + G$ queueing systems in Section 4.3.2.1. In the second part, a continuous adjustment of the interval length is developed in Section 4.3.2.2.

4.3.2.1 The stationary backlog-carryover approximation for systems with generally distributed abandonments

The SBC approximation for the time-dependent performance evaluation of $M(t)/M/c + G$ queueing systems divides the overall time horizon T into I intervals of length l_i ($i = 1, 2, ..., I$). For each interval, the input parameters are averaged. Then, each interval i is analyzed in two steps.

(1) In the first step, the corresponding stationary loss queueing system, i.e., an $M/M/c/c$ queueing system, is considered and the probability of blocking $P^{loss}_{block}(i)$ as well as the expected utilization $E[U^{loss}(i)]$ at the end of interval i are calculated according to

Equations (4.8) and (4.9) (Kleinrock (1975)).

$$P_{block}^{loss}(i) = \frac{\frac{\left(\frac{\tilde{\lambda}(i)}{\mu}\right)^c}{c!}}{\sum\limits_{n=0}^{c}\frac{\left(\frac{\tilde{\lambda}(i)}{\mu}\right)^n}{n!}} \tag{4.8}$$

$$E[U^{loss}(i)] = \frac{\tilde{\lambda}(i) \cdot \left(1 - P_{block}^{loss}(i)\right)}{c \cdot \mu} \tag{4.9}$$

Here, an artificial arrival rate $\tilde{\lambda}(i)$, given by Equation (4.11), is used as input that equals the sum of the actual arrival rate $\lambda(i)$ and a backlog rate of arrivals $b(i-1)$. This backlog includes arrivals that could not be served in the considered loss system of the previous interval and is calculated by multiplying the actual artificial arrival rate with the probability of blocking. Hence, dependencies between successive intervals are taken into account by carrying over non-served arrivals from an interval to the succeeding one.

As abandonments are customers that leave the system before being served, their occurrence results in a reduction of a systems' utilization. In order to consider this dependency in the SBC approach, the artificial arrival rate is reduced by the arrivals that will abandon in the actual or a later interval. These abandonments are calculated by multiplying the actual arrival rate $\lambda(i)$ with the probability to abandon $P_{abandon}(i)$. Hence the derivation of the artificial arrival rate results in

$$\tilde{\lambda}(i) = \lambda(i) - \lambda(i) \cdot P_{abandon}(i) + b(i-1). \tag{4.10}$$

However, when performing the first step of the SBC approach for interval i, the respective probability of abandonment $P_{abandon}(i)$ is not known. It is therefore approximated using the probability of abandonment $P_{abandon}(i-1)$ of the previous interval which results in

$$\tilde{\lambda}(i) = \lambda(i) - \lambda(i) \cdot P_{abandon}(i-1) + b(i-1)$$
$$= \lambda(i) \cdot (1 - P_{abandon}(i-1))$$
$$+\tilde{\lambda}(i-1) \cdot P_{block}^{loss}(i-1). \tag{4.11}$$

(2) The original stationary $M/M/c + G$ waiting system is considered in the second step of the SBC approach. It is used to calculate the different performance measures for interval i using a modified arrival rate $\lambda^{MAR}(i)$ as input. This modified arrival rate is chosen such that the utilization according to the stationary waiting system equals the utilization of the loss system considered in the first step of the SBC (Equation (4.12)). Here again, a time shift in the probability of abandonment has to be considered.

$$\lambda^{MAR}(i) = \frac{c \cdot \mu \cdot E[U^{loss}(i)]}{1 - P_{abandon}(i-1)} \tag{4.12}$$

The modified arrival rate $\lambda^{MAR}(i)$ is then used as input in a stationary $M/M/c + G$ queueing system to calculate the performance at the end of interval i. We use the approach of Zeltyn and Mandelbaum (2005) that calculates the exact performance measurements and allows for any arbitrarily distributed abandonments as long as the underlying distribution function G and survival function $\bar{G} = 1 - G$ are known.

In order to derive the performance at the end of interval i, the building blocks $J(i)$ and $J_H(i)$ have to be calculated (Equations (4.14) and (4.15)) using $H(x)$ as defined by Equation (4.13). Finally, the value $\epsilon(i)$ has to be introduced according to Equation (4.16).

$$H(x) = \int_0^x \bar{G}(u)\,du \tag{4.13}$$

105

$$J(i) = \int_0^\infty e^{\left(\lambda^{MAR}(i)H(x) - c\mu x\right)} dx \qquad (4.14)$$

$$J_H(i) = \int_0^\infty H(x) \cdot e^{\left(\lambda^{MAR}(i)H(x) - c\mu x\right)} dx \qquad (4.15)$$

$$\epsilon(i) = \frac{\sum_{j=0}^{c-1} \frac{1}{j!} \cdot \left(\frac{\lambda^{MAR}(i)}{\mu}\right)^j}{\frac{1}{(c-1)!} \cdot \left(\frac{\lambda^{MAR}(i)}{\mu}\right)^{c-1}} \qquad (4.16)$$

After the calculation of the building blocks, the expected queue length $E[L^Q(i)]$ and the expected waiting time of an item in the system $E[W^Q(i)]$ are calculated according to Equations (4.17) and (4.18), respectively.

$$E[L^Q(i)] = \frac{\left(\lambda^{MAR}(i)\right)^2 \cdot J_H(i)}{\epsilon + \lambda^{MAR}(i) \cdot J(i)} \qquad (4.17)$$

$$E[W^Q(i)] = \frac{\lambda^{MAR}(i) \cdot J_H}{\epsilon + \lambda^{MAR}(i) \cdot J} \qquad (4.18)$$

The expected utilization $E[U(i)]$ of the system is calculated using Equation (4.19). Equation (4.20) allows the derivation of the probability of abandonment $P_{abandon}(i)$.

$$E[U(i)] = \frac{\lambda^{MAR}(i) \cdot \left(1 - P_{abandon}(i)\right)}{c \cdot \mu} \qquad (4.19)$$

$$P_{abandon}(i) = \frac{1 + \left(\lambda^{MAR}(i) - c\mu\right) \cdot J(i)}{\epsilon + \lambda^{MAR}(i) \cdot J(i)} \qquad (4.20)$$

4.3.2.2 Continuous adjustment of the interval length

The traditional SBC approximation according to Stolletz (2008a) uses a constant interval length l_i that equals the length of the expected service time, i.e.,

$$l_i = \frac{1}{\mu} \qquad\qquad i = 1, 2, ..., I. \qquad (4.21)$$

In contrast, Stolletz and Lagershausen (2013) suggest to continuously adjust the interval length based on the utilization of the loss system considered in the first step of the SBC approach. They apply an adjustment according to Equation (4.22).

$$l_i = \frac{1}{\mathrm{E}[U^{loss}(i)]^2} \cdot \frac{1}{\mu} \qquad\qquad i = 1, 2, ..., I \qquad (4.22)$$

When using such a continuous adjustment, the artificial arrival rate given in Equation (4.11) has to be calibrated in order to account for a changing interval length in successive intervals, see Equation (4.23).

$$\tilde{\lambda}(i) = \lambda(i) \cdot (1 - P_{abandon}(i-1)) + b(i-1) \cdot \frac{l_{i-1}}{l_i} \qquad (4.23)$$

However, as the interval length l_i is already needed to derive the utilization of the loss system $\mathrm{E}[U^{loss}(i)]$, the first step of the SBC approach is performed twice. In the first run, the interval length of the previous interval is used as input in the derivation of the artificial arrival rate. Based on the resulting utilization, the final interval length is determined and the first step of the SBC approach is performed again.

Figures 4.3 and 4.4 show the transient behavior of the expected queue length $\mathrm{E}[L^Q(t)]$ in an $M/M/5 + M$ queueing system with a service rate of $\mu = 1.0$, as well as traffic intensities of $\rho = 0.9$ and $\rho = 1.5$, respectively. They include the performance according to the SBC approximation for different abandonment rates $\nu \in \{0.5, 1.0, 1.5\}$ using a constant interval length (fix) and an online adjustment according to Stolletz and Lagershausen (2013) (var). The solutions of the CKE (see Section 4.3.1) are used as benchmark for the approximation quality.

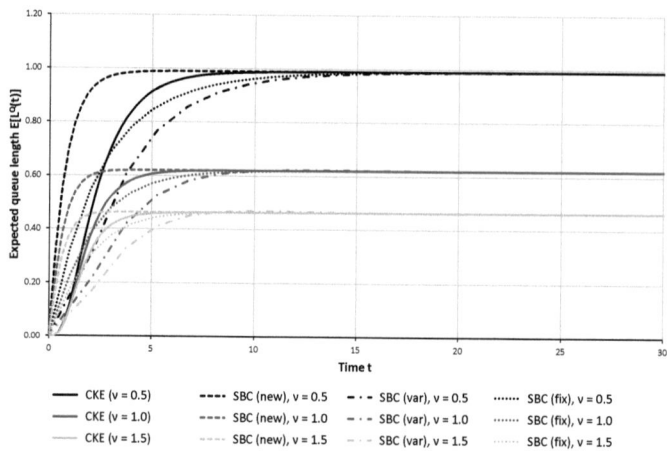

Figure 4.3: Interval length adjustment for an $M/M/5 + M$ system with $\rho = 0.9$

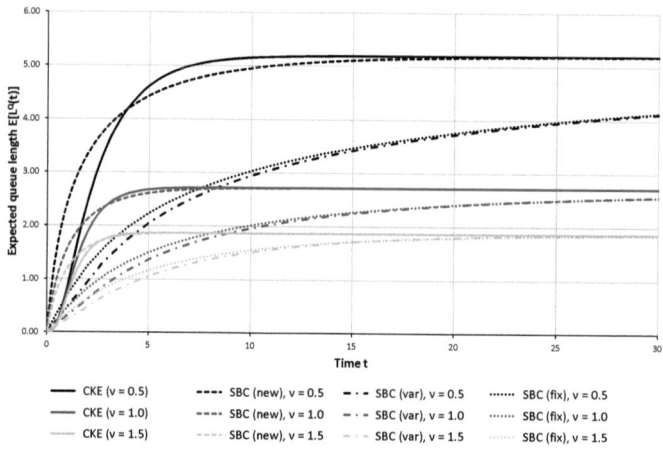

Figure 4.4: Interval length adjustment for an $M/M/5 + M$ system with $\rho = 1.5$

Both versions of the SBC approximation deliver a satisfying approximation quality in case of a traffic intensity of $\rho = 0.9$. However, in case of larger traffic intensities, the performance according to these versions lags behind and the interval length has to be smaller than the expected service time. Hence, the dependency given in Equation (4.24) turned out to be an appropriate rule for adjusting the interval length based on the loss system's utilization. The resulting performance using this rule for the continuous adjustment of the interval length is included in Figures 4.3 and 4.4, as well (new).

$$l_i = \left(1 - \mathrm{E}[U^{loss}(i)]\right) \cdot \frac{1}{\mu} \qquad (4.24)$$

The pseudo code describing the SBC approximation for $M(t)/M/c + G$ queueing systems incorporating a continuous adjustment of the interval length is given in Algorithm 4.1.

Algorithm 4.1 SBC approach

1: Input: $\lambda(i)$, c, μ, ν
2: Initialization: $b(0) = 0$, $P_{abandon}(0) = 0$, $l_0 = \frac{1}{\mu}$
3: **for** $i = 1$ **to** I **do**
4:      $\tilde{\lambda}(i) = \lambda(i) \cdot (1 - P_{abandon}(i-1)) + b(i-1)$
5:      **procedure** STATIONARY $M/M/c/c$ QUEUEING SYSTEM($\tilde{\lambda}(i)$, c, μ)
6:          **return** $\mathrm{E}[U^{loss}(i)]$
7:      **end procedure**
8:      $l_i = (1 - \mathrm{E}[U^{loss}(i)]) \cdot \frac{1}{\mu}$
9:      $\tilde{\lambda}(i) = \lambda(i) \cdot (1 - P_{abandon}(i-1)) + b(i-1) \cdot \frac{l_{i-1}}{l_i}$
10:      **procedure** STATIONARY $M/M/c/c$ QUEUEING SYSTEM($\tilde{\lambda}(i)$, c, μ)
11:          **return** $P_{block}^{loss}(i)$, $\mathrm{E}[U^{loss}(i)]$
12:      **end procedure**
13:      $b(i) = \tilde{\lambda}(i) \cdot P_{block}^{loss}(i)$
14:      $\lambda^{MAR}(i) = c \cdot \mu \cdot \mathrm{E}[U^{loss}(i)]$
15:      **procedure** STATIONARY $M/M/c + G$ QUEUEING SYSTEM($\lambda^{MAR}(i)$, c, μ, ν)
16:          **return** $P_{abandon}(i)$, $\mathrm{E}[U(i)]$, $\mathrm{E}[L^Q(i)]$, $\mathrm{E}[L^S(i)]$, $\mathrm{E}[W^Q(i)]$, $\mathrm{E}[W^S(i)]$
17:      **end procedure**
18: **end for**

4.3.3 The modified offered load approach

The MOL approximation was introduced by Jagerman (1975). Similar to the SBC approach described in Section 4.3.2, the MOL approach uses steady-state models to approximate the time-dependent performance of a queueing system at time t based on a modified arrival rate $\lambda^{MAR}(t)$.

The performance evaluation for an $M(t)/M/c$ queueing system according to the MOL approach works as follows. In an $M(t)/M/\infty$ queueing system, the expected number $L^S(t) = L^B(t)$ of busy servers at time t is described by the differential equation given by Equation (4.25). The solution of this differential equation is known.

$$E[L^B(t)]' = \lambda(t) - \mu \cdot E[L^B(t)] \qquad (4.25)$$

The modified arrival rate $\lambda^{MAR}(t)$ is now chosen such that the expected number of busy servers in the stationary $M/M/c$ queueing system equals the expected number of busy servers in the infinite server system (Equation (4.26)).

$$
\begin{aligned}
\frac{\lambda^{MAR}(t)}{\mu} &= E[L^B(t)] \\
\rightarrow \quad \lambda^{MAR}(t) &= E[L^B(t)] \cdot \mu \\
&= \int_{-\infty}^{t} \mu \cdot e^{-\mu \cdot (t-u)} \cdot \lambda(u) \cdot du \qquad (4.26)
\end{aligned}
$$

Finally, the modified arrival rate $\lambda^{MAR}(t)$ is used as input in the calculation of the performance at time t using standard steady-state formulas. The MOL approach for the analysis of queueing systems including abandonments works in a similar way. The only difference lies in the last step. Here, the modified arrival rate is used as input in the performance calculation according to a stationary queueing systems that includes abandonments (Feldman et al. (2008)). Similar to our implementation of the SBC approximation, we use the approach of Zeltyn and Mandelbaum (2005) to calculate the stationary performance of an $M/M/c + G$ queueing system as described in Section 4.3.2.1.

4.4 Limit result for stationary parameters

Even though, the SBC approximation described in Section 4.3.2 is developed for time-dependent parameters, an indicator of the approximation quality is the behavior of the approach in the limit. Preliminary analysis shows that the performance according to the SBC approximation converges to a steady state for stationary parameters if time goes to infinity. Moreover, such a behavior has been proven for the SBC approximation for $M/M/c$ queueing systems by Stolletz (2008a).

In the following, we show for constant input parameters that if the performance resulting from the SBC approximation converges to a steady state, it converges to the performance according to the underlying steady-state model. This is done analytically by deducing that the modified arrival rate $\lambda^{MAR}(i)$ converges to a stationary value λ^{MAR} that equals the stationary input arrival rate λ. If this relation holds, all performance measures, that are derived using this arrival rate as input, converge as well.

Let us assume that the SBC approach converges to a steady state and that λ, $\tilde{\lambda}$, λ^{MAR}, P_{block}^{loss}, $E[U^{loss}]$, and $P_{abandon}$ denote the corresponding stationary values. Applying the limit $i \to \infty$ to the calculation of the utilization of the loss system in the first step of the SBC approach results in Equation (4.27).

$$
\begin{aligned}
\lim_{i \to \infty} E[U^{loss}(i)] &= \lim_{i \to \infty} \frac{\tilde{\lambda}(i) \cdot \left(1 - P_{block}^{loss}(i)\right)}{c \cdot \mu} \\
&= \lim_{i \to \infty} \frac{\tilde{\lambda}(i) - b(i)}{c \cdot \mu}
\end{aligned}
\tag{4.27}
$$

In steady state, the backlog and the interval length in succeeding intervals do not change, i.e., $b(i) = b(i-1)$ and $l_i = l_{i-1}$. Hence, incorporating the calculation of the artificial arrival rate according to Equation (4.11) in

Equation (4.27) leads to Equation (4.28).

$$\lim_{i \to \infty} E[U^{loss}(i)]$$

$$= \lim_{i \to \infty} \frac{\lambda(i) \cdot (1 - P_{abandon}(i-1)) + b(i-1) \cdot \frac{l_{i-1}}{l_i} - b(i)}{c \cdot \mu}$$

$$= \lim_{i \to \infty} \frac{\lambda(i) \cdot (1 - P_{abandon}(i-1))}{c \cdot \mu}$$

$$= \frac{\lambda \cdot (1 - P_{abandon})}{c \cdot \mu}$$

$$= E[U^{loss}] \tag{4.28}$$

Based on Equation (4.28), the actual arrival rate λ can be calculated according to Equation (4.29).

$$\lambda = \frac{c \cdot \mu \cdot E[U^{loss}]}{1 - P_{abandon}} \tag{4.29}$$

Applying the limit $i \to \infty$ to the calculation of the modified arrival rate according to Equation (4.12) results in Equation (4.30).

$$\lim_{i \to \infty} \lambda^{MAR}(i) = \lim_{i \to \infty} \frac{c \cdot \mu \cdot E[U^{loss}(i)]}{1 - P_{abandon}(i)} \tag{4.30}$$

$$\Leftrightarrow \quad \lambda^{MAR}(i) = \frac{c \cdot \mu \cdot E[U^{loss}]}{1 - P_{abandon}} \tag{4.31}$$

It can be seen from Equations (4.29) and (4.31) that the modified arrival rate converges to the actual arrival rate if i goes to infinity. Hence, the performance according to the SBC (using a stationary model and the modified arrival rate as input) converges to the performance of the steady-state model using the actual arrival rate as input.

4.5 Numerical study

The numerical study to analyze the performance evaluation of queueing systems with abandonments by means of the SBC approximation and the MOL approach consists of three parts. While Section 4.5.1 deals with exponentially distributed abandonments, generally and non-Markovian distributed abandonments are considered in Section 4.5.2. The last part of the numerical study includes the performance analysis of a real-world call center by means of the SBC approach in Section 4.5.3.

4.5.1 Markovian abandonments

This subsection deals with the performance evaluation of $M(t)/M/c+M$ queueing systems with exponentially distributed abandonment times. The examples of Subsections 4.5.1 and 4.5.2 use artificial data and assume a time-dependent arrival process that results in the time-dependent traffic intensity $\rho(t) = \lambda(t)/(c \cdot \mu)$ given in Figure 4.5. It contains several steps and different intensity levels including periods of significant overload with a maximum traffic intensity of $\rho(t) = 1.5$ for $65 \leq t \leq 70$.

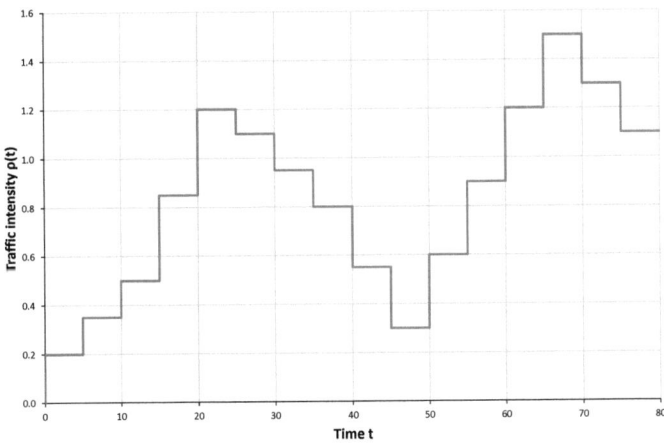

Figure 4.5: Time-dependent traffic intensity

The performance evaluation is performed using the SBC approximation described in Section 4.3.2, the MOL approach described in Section 4.3.3, and the stationary independent period-by-period (SIPP) approximation. The SIPP approach derives the performance at time t by using a stationary model and the instantaneous arrival rate $\lambda(t)$ as input (Green et al. (2001)). Thus, it ignores any transient behavior and all dependencies between consecutive time intervals. The solution of the CKE (see Section 4.3.1) for this system serves as benchmark for the approximation quality.

First of all, an $M(t)/M/5 + M$ queueing system with $c = 5$ servers, a service rate of $\mu = 1.0$, and an abandonment rate of $\nu = 0.5$ is considered. Applying an arrival rate according to the traffic intensity given in Figure 4.5, the resulting expected time-dependent utilization $\mathrm{E}[U(t)]$ is given in Figure 4.6. Accordingly, Figure 4.7 includes the expected time-dependent number of items in the system $\mathrm{E}[L^S(t)]$.

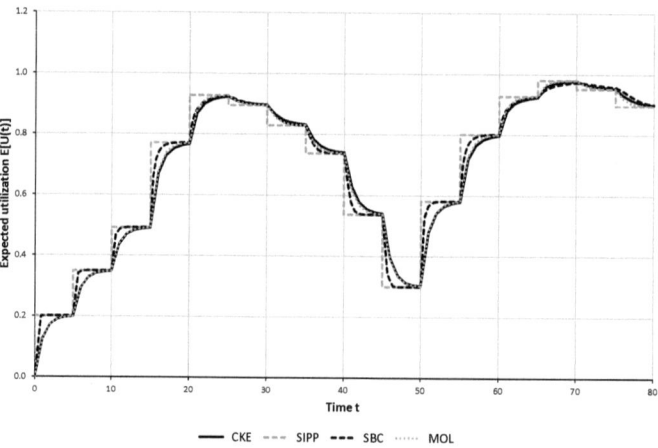

Figure 4.6: Expected utilization $\mathrm{E}[U(t)]$ in an $M(t)/M/5 + M$ system ($\nu = 0.5$)

In contrast to the SIPP approximation, the SBC approximation and the MOL approach consider the time-dependent behavior within periods with

114

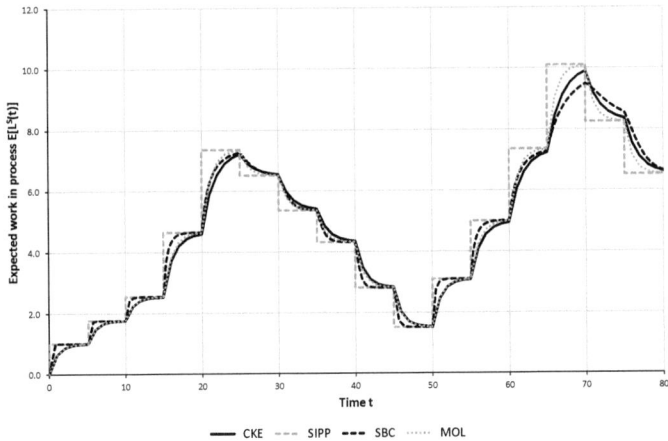

Figure 4.7: Expected work in process $\mathrm{E}[L^S(t)]$ in an $M(t)/M/5 + M$ system ($\nu = 0.5$)

constant input arrival rate. Figures 4.6 and 4.7 indicate that both approaches deliver good approximation results for a wide range of traffic intensities including periods of overload and underload. The approximation quality of the MOL approach increases with decreasing traffic intensity. The accuracy of the SBC approach increases as the traffic intensity approaches critically loaded periods, i.e., periods with $\rho(t) \approx 1$. In general, the approximation quality of the MOL approach outperforms the SBC approximation.

Figure 4.8 includes the expected time-dependent queue length $\mathrm{E}[L^Q(t)]$ in an $M(t)/M/5 + M$ queueing system with an increased abandonment rate of $\nu = 1.5$. Here, the accuracy of the MOL approach and the SBC approximation as well as their qualitative behavior are similar to the case of a smaller abandonment rate described in the previous paragraph.

115

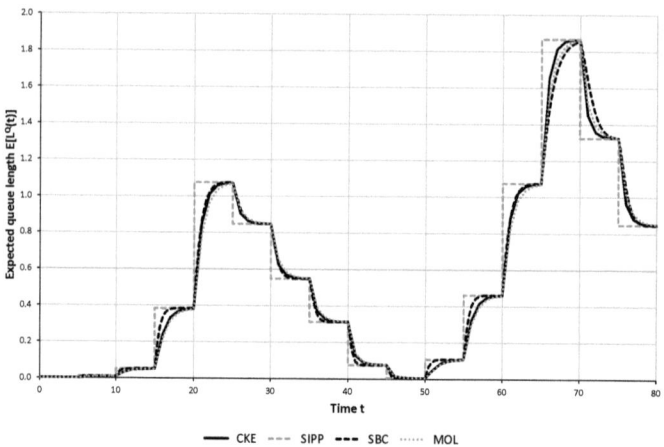

Figure 4.8: Expected queue length $E[L^Q(t)]$ in an $M(t)/M/5 + M$ system ($\nu = 1.5$)

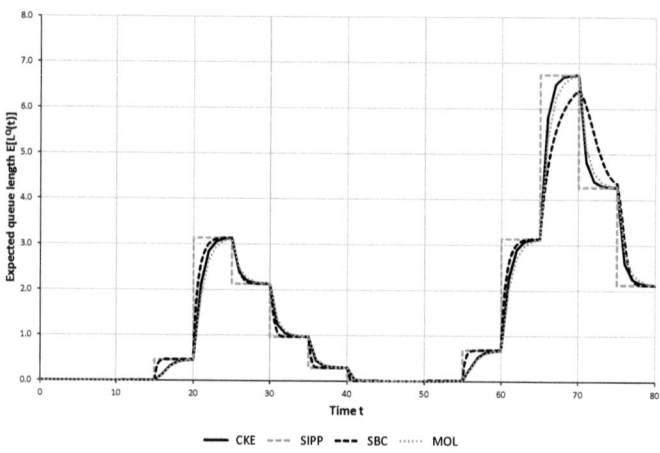

Figure 4.9: Expected queue length $E[L^Q(t)]$ in an $M(t)/M/20 + M$ system ($\nu = 1.5$)

Figure 4.9 depicts the expected time-dependent queue length in a larger $M(t)/M/20 + M$ queueing system with a service rate of $\mu = 1.0$ and a high abandonment rate of $\nu = 1.5$. Even though the approximation

116

quality of the SBC approximation is not as good as in the system with $c = 5$ parallel servers, it still delivers good approximation results that improve when approaching critically loaded periods. In this case, the MOL approach outperforms the SBC approximation, too.

Even though the presented results include only a single performance measure in each case, the results and insights are the same for other performance measures as they are derived using the identical modified arrival rate as input.

4.5.2 Generally distributed abandonments

Section 4.5.2 aims at demonstrating the applicability of the SBC approximation and the MOL approach to queueing systems that incorporate generally distributed abandonments. An $M(t)/M/10 + G$ queueing system with $c = 10$ parallel servers and a service rate of $\mu = 1.0$ is considered. In accordance to Section 4.5.1, the time-dependent arrival rate is chosen such that it results in the time-dependent traffic intensity given in Figure 4.5. For an abandonment rate of $\nu = 1.5$, we assume deterministic, uniformly distributed, or Gamma distributed abandonment times. Thus, the abandonment times vary within the interval $[\frac{1}{3}, 1]$ in case of uniformly distributed abandonments (coefficient of variation $CV = 0.2887$). In case of Gamma distributed abandonments, the shape parameter equals $k = 2.0$ and the scale parameter is set to $\theta = \frac{1}{\nu \cdot k} = \frac{1}{3}$ ($CV = 0.7071$).

The resulting expected time-dependent queue length $\mathrm{E}[L^Q(t)]$ is given in Figures 4.10 to 4.12, respectively. As the solution of the CKE is not applicable to systems with generally distributed abandonments, the results of simulations with 1,000,000 replications are used as benchmarks.

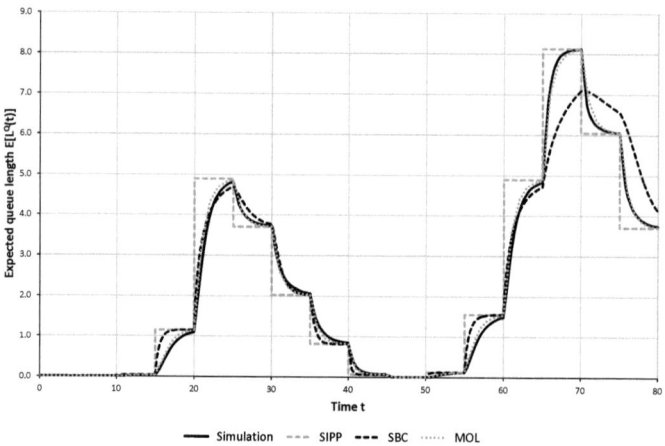

Figure 4.10: Expected queue length $\mathrm{E}[L^Q(t)]$ in an $M(t)/M/10+D$ system

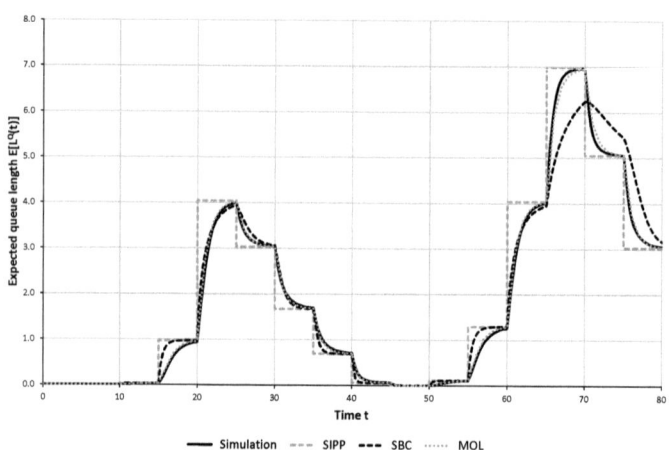

Figure 4.11: Expected queue length $\mathrm{E}[L^Q(t)]$ in an $M(t)/M/10+G$ system with uniformly distributed abandonments

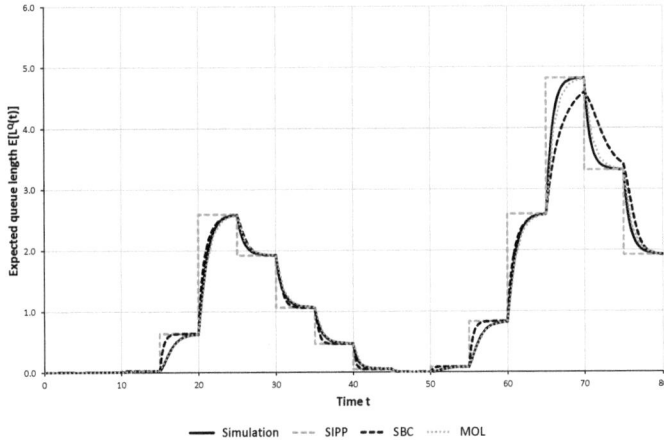

Figure 4.12: Expected queue length $E[L^Q(t)]$ in an $M(t)/M/10+G$ system with Gamma distributed abandonments

Besides the expected utilization, the expected queue length, and the expected work in process, both the SBC approximation and the MOL approach enable the possibility to approximate additional performance measures such as the expected time-dependent waiting time of an item and the time-dependent probability of abandonment, i.e., the probability that an item leaves the system before being served. Hence, Figure 4.13 includes the expected time-dependent waiting time $E[W^Q(t)]$ of an item in the system with uniformly distributed abandonments. The time-dependent probability of abandonment $P_{abandon}(t)$ in the system featuring Gamma distributed abandonments is depicted in Figure 4.14.

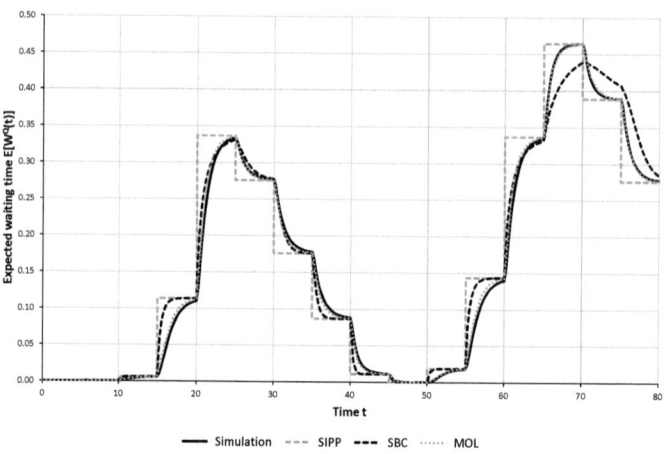

Figure 4.13: Expected waiting time $E[W^Q(t)]$ in an $M(t)/M/10 + G$ system with uniformly distributed abandonments

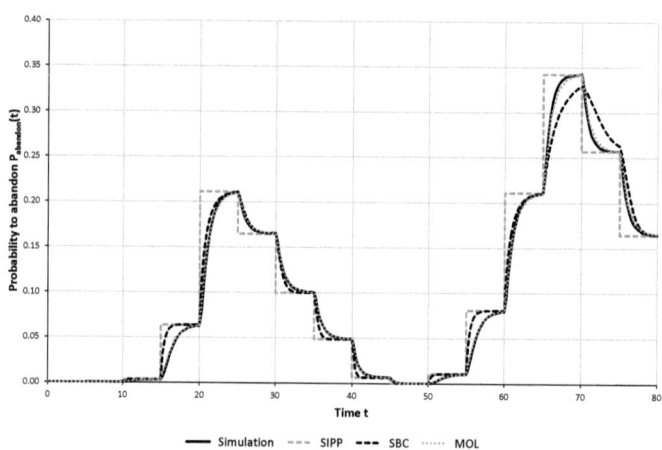

Figure 4.14: Probability of abandonment $P_{abandon}(t)$ in an $M(t)/M/10 + G$ system with Gamma distributed abandonments

Figures 4.10 to 4.14 indicate that the MOL approach delivers a good approximation quality that outperforms the SBC approximation. Nonetheless, the SBC approach still delivers good approximation results for queueing systems with abandonments that follow different general distributions. Similar to Markovian systems, the accuracy of the SBC approach improves when the traffic intensity approaches critically loaded periods.

4.5.3 Real-world system

In the following, we consider a real-world call center of a small bank in Israel. The data are provided by the Faculty of Industrial Engineering and Management at the Technion in Haifa (Technion (2000)). It contains all information about the inbound calls for the whole year 1999. The banking facility can be modeled as an $M(t)/M/c + G$ queueing system. The service rate per agent equals $\mu = 0.3133$ calls per minute. Assuming constant arrival rates within 15 minutes intervals, the time-dependent arrival rate is shown in Figure 4.15. It is based on mean values over all calls on weekdays.

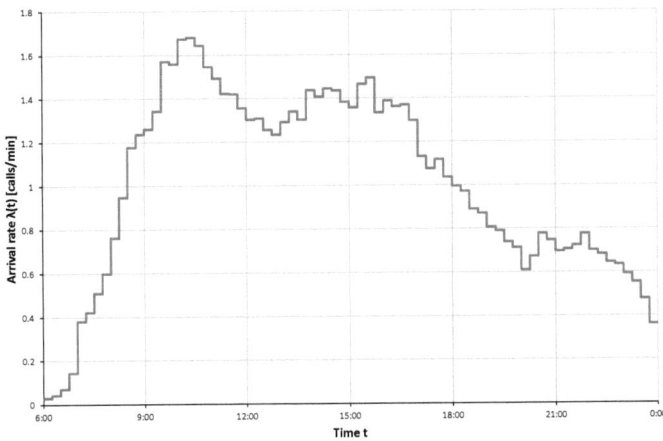

Figure 4.15: Arrival rate $\lambda(t)$ of calls

The patience of the calling customers follows a general distribution whose frequencies are given in Figure 4.16. This distribution includes two peaks.

One peak occurs directly at zero seconds and refers to customers that are not willing to wait at all and hang up if not served immediately. A second peak occurs after 15 seconds. Even though in the numerical example, abandonment times up to 15 minutes are considered, Figure 4.16 is restricted to 2 minutes for the purpose of presentation.

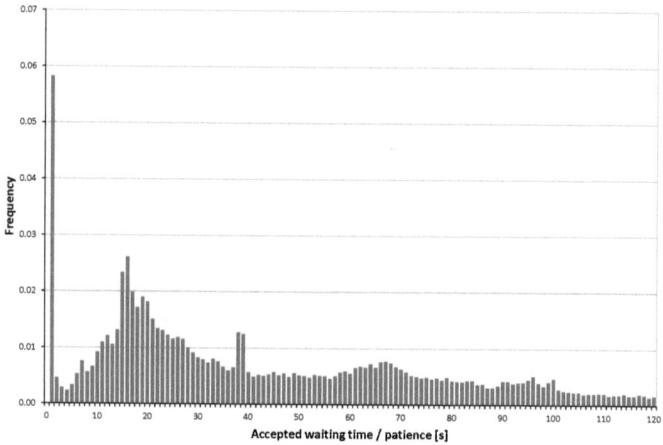

Figure 4.16: Distribution of the abandonment times

The data include no information on the number of agents working in parallel. Thus, in several experiments, we derive the performance measures of the banking facility for $c = 3$ up to $c = 7$ parallel telephone agents. As the data do not provide any performance measures of the system, we use the results of simulations with 1,000,000 replications as benchmark for the accuracy of our SBC approximation.

The expected time-dependent utilization $E[U(t)]$, the expected time-dependent waiting time of a call in the queue $E[W^Q(t)]$, and the time-dependent probability of abandonment $P_{abandon}(t)$ are presented in Figures 4.17 to 4.19, respectively, for the time between 08:00 and 12:00 and the different settings with $c \in \{3, 4, 5, 6, 7\}$ agents working in parallel.

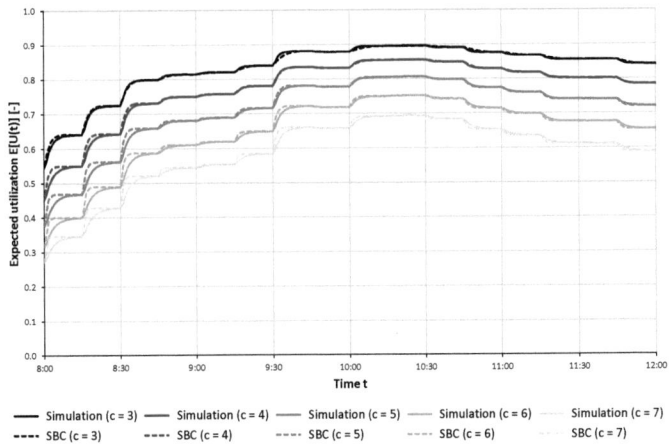

Figure 4.17: Expected utilization $E[U(t)]$ of the system based on real-world data

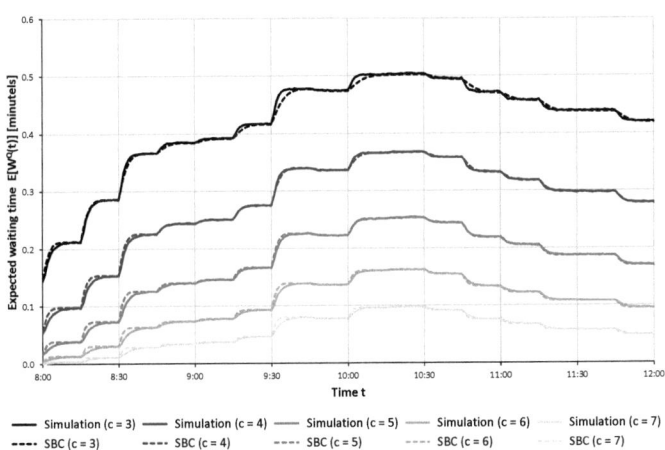

Figure 4.18: Expected waiting time $E[W^Q(t)]$ in the system based on real-world data

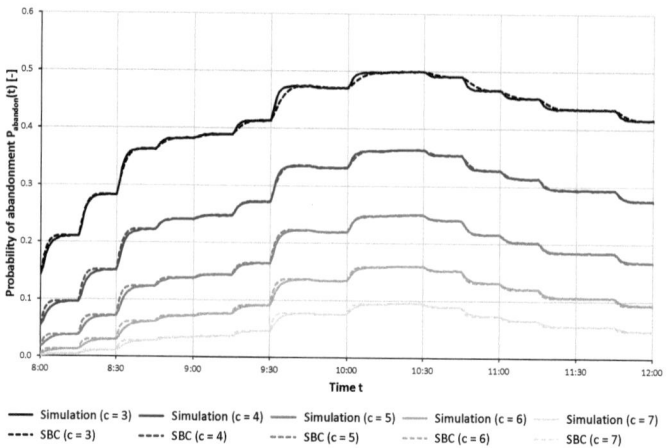

Figure 4.19: Probability of abandonment $P_{abandon}(t)$ of the system based on real-world data

As expected, the expected utilization, the expected waiting time, and the probability of abandonment decrease with an increasing number of telephone agents working in parallel. All three figures reveal that the SBC approach delivers a good performance approximation for the real-world case that includes generally distributed abandonment times. The approximation quality of the SBC approach increases with higher utilization of the system.

4.6 Conclusion

Queueing systems are often characterized by impatient customers that leave the queue without being served. In this paper, an SBC approximation is derived for the performance evaluation of $M(t)/M/c + G$ queueing systems that feature a time-dependent arrival rate and generally distributed abandonment times. In a numerical study, we show its applicability to a wide range of system configurations, including different numbers of servers as well as large fluctuations in the traffic intensity and compare the approximation results to those of the MOL approach. Additionally, the possible usage of the approaches for different distributions of the abandonment times is delineated. Finally, the SBC approximation is applied to the performance evaluation of a real-world call center.

Fields for future research include possible extensions to the considered queueing system. Hence, e.g., generally distributed service times or abandoning customers that re-enter the system after some time, so-called re-trials, could be considered. In this work, the continuous adjustment of the interval length in the SBC approach is motivated by numerical observations. Thus, a theoretical foundation would be an interesting issue and could lead to an improvement of accuracy. As the SBC approximation targets only the performance evaluation of queueing systems with abandonments, the integration of the SBC approach into optimization approaches could be promising.

5 Conclusions and outlook

5.1 Conclusions

The three essays of this dissertation deal with methods for the non-stationary performance evaluation of queueing systems with time-dependent input parameters. The survey in Chapter 2 gives a structured overview of the literature on approaches for the analysis of single-stage queueing systems. It includes a new classification scheme which categorizes the different approaches based on the underlying key idea. In addition to the description of the methodologies and the classification of the relevant literature, methodological links between different approaches are illustrated. Thus, for example, the SBC approximation and the MOL approach are classified into different categories even though they share the common idea of using a modified arrival rate as input in the performance calculation by means of stationary models. The last part of the survey reveals that the performance analysis of time-dependent queueing systems has a wide range of areas of application. Nevertheless, it also shows that most evaluation methods are mainly used within a specific area of application. For example, the CTT is used only for the analysis of road traffic systems.

Chapters 3 and 4 are dedicated to the derivation of approaches for the performance evaluation of queueing systems with specific system characteristics. In Chapter 3, an SBC approximation is derived that allows for the analysis of a real-world truck handling system that consists of two parallel single-stage queueing systems. Furthermore, the system includes a routing decision at each truck's arrival that depends on the current state of the system. A numerical study shows the good approximation quality of the SBC approach by comparison with the SIPP approach and simulation results as benchmark. In addition to artificial data, the applicability of the SBC approximation to real-world data including phases of under- and overload is delineated.

Chapter 4 deals with the performance evaluation of $M(t)/M/c + G$ queueing systems. It includes the derivation of a new SBC approximation and the implementation of the MOL approach by Jagerman (1975). Within a numerical study, the applicability of both approaches to a wide range of system configurations including deterministic, Markovian, uniform, and Gamma distributed abandonments is shown. Both approaches are compared to each other with respect to their approximation quality. Hereby, the solution of the Chapman-Kolmogorov equations is used as benchmark in case of Markovian abandonments and simulation results are used as benchmark, otherwise. Even though both approaches deliver good approximation results, the approximation accuracy of the MOL approach outperforms the SBC approximation in most cases. The last example of the numerical study shows the applicability of the SBC approximation for the performance evaluation of a real-world call center that includes abandonments following an arbitrary distribution.

5.2 Further possible research directions

The literature overview in Chapter 2 serves as a good basis for the identification of research gaps and open fields for further investigation. Thus, the integration of different approaches may be promising by combining the strength of different methodologies. This may result in new approaches that allow for the analysis of more general queueing systems or may result in approaches with an improved approximation accuracy to an extended range of system parameters including different levels and patterns of stochasticity. Even though the survey gives a substantial overview, it lacks a comprehensive numerical study that compares the various approaches with respect to their system-specific capabilities and their approximation accuracy.

The essays within this dissertation focus on approaches for the performance evaluation of queueing systems. However, they do not give decision support or include recommendations for possibly occurring issues. Thus, the integration of evaluation approaches in optimization procedures is a promising field for further research. This includes, for example, the implementation of a system to actively manage truck arrivals in order to improve the utilization and other performance measures of the truck handling system discussed in Chapter 3. With respect to Chapter 4, the integration of evaluation approaches into staffing algorithms may help to improve the performance of a call center.

Bibliography

Abol'nikov, L. M. (1968). A nonstationary queueing problem for a system with an infinite number of channels for a group arrival of requests. *Problems of Information Transmission 4*(3), 82–85.

Agnew, C. E. (1976). Dynamic Modeling and Control of Congestion-Prone Systems. *Operations Research 24*(3), 400–419.

Agnihothri, S. R. and P. F. Taylor (1991). Staffing a Centralized Appointment Scheduling Department in Lourdes Hospital. *Interfaces 21*(5), 1–11.

Aguir, S., F. Karaesmen, O. Z. Aksin, and F. Chauvet (2004). The impact of retrials on call center performance. *OR Spectrum 26*(3), 353–376.

Akgun, O. T., R. Righter, and R. Wolff (2012). Understanding the marginal impact of customer flexibility. *Queueing Systems 71*(1-2), 5–23.

Al-Seedy, R. O. and F. M. Al-Ibraheem (2003). New transient solution to the $M/M/\infty$ queue with varying arrival and departure rate. *Applied Mathematics and Computation 135*(2-3), 425–428.

Al-Seedy, R. O., A. A. El-Sherbiny, S. A. El-Shehawy, and S. I. Ammar (2009). The transient solution to a time-dependent single-server queue with balking. *The Mathematical Scientist 34*(2), 113–118.

Alfa, A. S. (1979). A Numerical Method for Evaluating Delay to a Customer in a Time-Inhomogeneous, Single Server Queue with Batch Arrivals. *The Journal of the Operational Research Society 30*(7), 665–667.

Alfa, A. S. (1982). Time-Inhomogenous Bulk Server Queue in Discrete Time: A Transportation Type Problem. *Operations Research 30*(4), 650–658.

Alfa, A. S. (1990). Approximating queue lengths in $M(t)/D/1$ queues. *European Journal of Operational Research 44*(1), 60–66.

Alfa, A. S. and M. Chen (1991). Approximating queue lengths in $M(t)/G/1$ queue using the maximum entropy principle. *Acta Informatica 28*(8), 801–815.

Alfa, A. S. and B. H. Margolius (2008). Two classes of time-inhomogeneous Markov chains: Analysis of the periodic case. *Annals of Operations Research 160*(1), 121–137.

Alnowibet, K. A. and H. Perros (2006). The Nonstationary Loss Queue: A Survey. In J. A. Barria (Ed.), *Communication Networks and Computer Systems - A Tribute to Professor Erol Gelenbe*, pp. 105–125. Imperial College Press.

Andrews, B. and H. Parsons (1993). Establishing Telephone-Agent Staffing Levels through Economic Optimization. *Interfaces 23*(2), 14–20.

Ansell, P. S., K. D. Glazebrook, J. Niño Mora, and M. O'Keeffe (2003). Whittle's index policy for a multi-class queueing system with convex holding costs. *Mathematical Methods of Operations Research (ZOR) 57*(1), 21–39.

Argon, N. T., L. Ding, K. D. Glazebrook, and S. Ziya (2009). Dynamic routing of customers with general delay costs in a multiserver queuing system. *Probability in the Engineering and Informational Sciences 23*(2), 175–203.

Arns, M., P. Buchholz, and A. Panchenko (2010). On the Numerical Analysis of Inhomogeneous Continuous-Time Markov Chains. *INFORMS Journal on Computing 22*(3), 416–432.

Atlason, J., M. A. Epelman, and S. G. Henderson (2008). Optimizing Call Center Staffing Using Simulation and Analytic Center Cutting-Plane Methods. *Management Science 54*(2), 295–309.

Bartodziej, P., U. Derigs, D. Malcherek, and U. Vogel (2009). Models and algorithms for solving combined vehicle and crew scheduling problems with rest constraints: An application to road feeder service planning in air cargo transportation. *OR Spectrum 31*(2), 405–429.

Bennett, J. C. and D. J. Worthington (1998). An Example of a Good but Partially Successful OR Engagement: Improving Outpatient Clinic Operations. *Interfaces 28*(5), 56–69.

Bertsimas, D. and X. V. Doan (2010). Robust and data-driven approaches to call centers. *European Journal of Operational Research 207*(2), 1072–1085.

Bertsimas, D. and G. Mourtzinou (1997). Transient laws of non-stationary queueing systems and their applications. *Queueing Systems 25*(1-4), 115–155.

Bhattacharjee, P. and P. K. Ray (2014). Patient flow modelling and performance analysis of healthcare delivery processes in hospitals: A review and reflections. *Computers & Industrial Engineering 78*, 299–312.

Blumberg-Nitzani, M. and H. Bar-Gera (2014). The effect of signalised intersections on dynamic traffic assignment solution stability. *Transportmetrica A: Transport Science 10*(7), 622–646.

Bookbinder, J. H. (1986). Multiple queues of aircraft under time-dependent conditions. *INFOR 24*(4), 280–288.

Bookbinder, J. H. and D. L. Martell (1979). Time-dependent queueing approach to helicopter allocation for forest fire initial-attack. *INFOR 17*(1), 58–70.

Brahimi, M. and D. J. Worthington (1991a). Queueing Models for Out-Patient Appointment Systems – A Case Study. *Journal of the Operational Research Society 42*(9), 733–746.

Brahimi, M. and D. J. Worthington (1991b). The finite capacity multi-server queue with inhomogeneous arrival rate and discrete service time distribution - and its application to continuous service time problems. *European Journal of Operational Research 50*(3), 310–324.

Brilon, W. and N. Wu (1990). Delays at fixed-time traffic signals under time-dependent traffic conditions. *Traffic Engineering & Control 31*(12), 623–631.

Brown, L., N. Gans, A. Mandelbaum, A. Sakov, H. Shen, S. Zeltyn, and L. Zhao (2005). Statistical Analysis of a Telephone Call Center: A Queueing-Science Perspective. *Journal of the American Statistical Association 100*(469), 36–50.

Brown, M. and S. M. Ross (1969). Some Results for Infinite Server Poisson Queues. *Journal of Applied Probability 6*(3), 604–611.

Buczkowski, P. S. and V. G. Kulkarni (2006). Funding a warranty reserve with contributions after each sale. *Probability in the Engineering and Informational Sciences 20*(3), 497–515.

Carrillo, M. J. (1991). Extensions of Palm's Theorem: A Review. *Management Science 37*(6), 739–744.

Catling, I. (1977). A time-dependent approach to junction delays. *Traffic Engineering & Control 18*(11), 520–526.

Chassioti, E., D. Worthington, and K. Glazebrook (2014). Effects of state-dependent balking on multi-server non-stationary queueing systems. *Journal of the Operational Research Society 65*(2), 278–290.

Chassioti, E. and D. J. Worthington (2004). A new model for call centre queue management. *Journal of the Operational Research Society 55*(12), 1352–1357.

Chen, G., K. Govindan, and M. M. Golias (2013). Reducing truck emissions at container terminals in a low carbon economy: Proposal of a queueing-based bi-objective model for optimizing truck arrival pattern. *Transportation Research Part E: Logistics and Transportation Review 55*, 3–22.

Chen, G., K. Govindan, and Z. Yang (2013). Managing truck arrivals with time windows to alleviate gate congestion at container terminals. *International Journal of Production Economics 141*(1), 179–188.

Chen, G., K. Govindan, Z.-Z. Yang, T.-M. Choi, and L. Jiang (2013). Terminal appointment system design by non-stationary $M(t)/E_k/c(t)$ queueing model and genetic algorithm. *International Journal of Production Economics 146*(2), 694–703.

Chen, G. and Z. Yang (2010). Optimizing time windows for managing export container arrivals at Chinese container terminals. *Martime Economics & Logistics 12*(1), 111–126.

Chen, G. and Z.-Z. Yang (2014). Methods for estimating vehicle queues at a marine terminal: A computational comparison. *International Journal of Applied Mathematics and Computer Science 24*(3), 611–619.

Chen, X., X. Zhou, and G. F. List (2011). Using time-varying tolls to optimize truck arrivals at ports. *Transportation Research Part E: Logistics and Transportation Review 47*(6), 965–982.

Choudhury, G. L., D. M. Lucantoni, and W. Whitt (1997). Numerical Solution of Piecewise-Stationary $M_t/G_t/1$ Queues. *Operations Research 45*(3), 451–463.

Chung, K. and D. Min (2014). Staffing a service system with appointment-based customer arrivals. *Journal of the Operational Research Society 65*(10), 1533–1543.

Clark, G. M. (1981). Use of Polya Distributions in Approximate Solutions to Nonstationary $M/M/s$ Queues. *Communications of the ACM 24*(4), 206–217.

Clarke, A. B. (1956). A Waiting Line Process of Markov Type. *The Annals of Mathematical Statistics 27*(2), 452–459.

Collings, T. and C. Stoneman (1976). The $M/M/\infty$ Queue with Varying Arrival and Departure Rates. *Operations Research 24*(4), 760–773.

Cosmetatos, G. P. (1976). Some Approximate Equilibrium Results for the Multi-Server Queue $(M/G/r)$. *Operational Research Quarterly 27*(3), 615–620.

Crabtree, T., J. Edgar, T. Hoang, R. Tom, and B. Hart (2012). World Air Cargo Forecast 2012-2013. Seattle: Boeing Commercial Airplanes.

Creemers, S., M. Defraeye, and I. van Nieuwenhuyse (2014). G-RAND: A phase-type approximation for the nonstationary $G(t)/G(t)/s(t) + G(t)$ queue. *Performance Evaluation 80*, 102–123.

Curry, G. L., A. De Vany, and R. M. Feldman (1978). A queueing model of airport passenger departures by taxi: Competition with a public transportation mode. *Transportation Research 12*(2), 115–120.

Czachórski, T., K. Grochla, T. Nycz, and F. Pekergin (2010). A diffusion approximation model for wireless networks based on IEEE 802.11 standard. *Computer Communications 33*, S86–S92.

Czachórski, T., T. Nycz, and F. Pekergin (2009). Diffusion Approximation Models for Transient States and their Application to Priority Queues. *International Journal On Advances in Networks and Services 2*(2&3), 205–217.

Dai, L. (1998). Performance Bounds for Nonhomogeneous Queues. *IEEE Transactions on Automatic Control 43*(5), 700–705.

Daniel, J. I. (1995). Congestion Pricing and Capacity of Large Hub Airports: A Bottleneck Model with Stochastic Queues. *Econometrica 63*(2), 327–370.

Daniel, J. I. and K. T. Harback (2008). (When) Do hub airlines internalize their self-imposed congestion delays? *Journal of Urban Economics 63*(2), 583–612.

Daniel, J. I. and K. T. Harback (2009). Pricing the major US hub airports. *Journal of Urban Economics 66*(1), 33–56.

Daniel, J. I. and M. Pahwa (2000). Comparison of Three Empirical Models of Airport Congestion Pricing. *Journal of Urban Economics 47*(1), 1–38.

De Barros, A. G. and D. D. Tomber (2007). Quantitative Analysis of Passenger and Baggage Security Screening at Airports. *Journal of Advanced Transportation 41*(2), 171–193.

De Bruin, A. M., A. C. van Rossum, M. C. Visser, and G. M. Koole (2007). Modeling the emergency cardiac in-patient flow: an application of queuing theory. *Health Care Management Science 10*(2), 125–137.

de Neufville, R. and M. Grillot (1982). Design of Pedestrian Space in Airport Terminals. *Transportation Engineering Journal of ASCE 108*(1), 87–102.

Defraeye, M. and I. Van Nieuwenhuyse (2011). Setting staffing levels in an emergency department: opportunities and limitations of stationary queueing models. *Review of Business and Economics 56*(1), 73 – 100.

Defraeye, M. and I. Van Nieuwenhuyse (2016). Staffing and scheduling under nonstationary demand for service: A literature review. *Omega 58*, 4–25.

Deng, C. C., H. L. Ong, B. W. Ang, and T. N. Goh (1992). A Modelling Study of a Taxi Service Operation. *International Journal of Operations & Production Management 12*(11), 65–78.

Di Crescenzo, A. and A. G. Nobile (1995). Diffusion approximation to a queueing system with time-dependent arrival and service rates. *Queueing Systems 19*(1-2), 41–62.

Dietz, D. C. (2011). Practical scheduling for call center operations. *Omega 39*(5), 550–557.

Dietz, D. C. and J. G. Vaver (2006). Synergistic modeling of call center operations. *Journal of Applied Mathematics and Decision Sciences 2006*(2), 1–13.

Dormand, J. R. and P. J. Prince (1980). A family of embedded Runge-Kutta formulae. *Journal of Computational and Applied Mathematics 6*(1), 19–26.

Dormuth, D. W. and A. S. Alfa (1997). Two finite-difference methods for solving $MAP(t)/PH(t)/1/K$ queueing models. *Queueing Systems 27*(1-2), 55–78.

Duda, A. (1986). Diffusion Approximations for Time-Dependent Queueing Systems. *IEEE Journal on Selected Areas in Communications 4*(6), 905–918.

Eick, S. G., W. A. Massey, and W. Whitt (1993a). $M_t/G/\infty$ Queues with Sinusoidal Arrival Rates. *Management Science 39*(2), 241–252.

Eick, S. G., W. A. Massey, and W. Whitt (1993b). The Physics of the $M_t/G/\infty$ Queue. *Operations Research 41*(4), 731–742.

El-Sherbiny, A. A. (2010). Transient Solution to an infinite Server Queue with Varying Arrival and Departure Rate. *Journal of Mathematics and Statistics 6*(1), 1–3.

Ellis, P. M. (2010). The Time-Dependent Mean and Variance of the Non-Stationary Markovian Infinite Server System. *Journal of Mathematics and Statistics 6*(1), 68–71.

Escobar, M., A. R. Odoni, and E. Roth (2002). Approximate solution for multi-server queueing systems with Erlangian service times. *Computers & Operations Research 29*(10), 1353–1374.

Feldman, Z., A. Mandelbaum, W. A. Massey, and W. Whitt (2008). Staffing of Time-Varying Queues to Achieve Time-Stable Performance. *Management Science 54*(2), 324–338.

Filipiak, J. (1983). Diffusion-equation model of slightly loaded $M/M/1$ queue. *Operations Research Letters 2*(3), 134–139.

Filipiak, J. (1984). Dynamic Routing in a Queueing System with a Multiple Service Facility. *Operations Research 32*(5), 1163–1180.

Flick, A. and M. Liao (2010). A queuing system with time varying rates. *Statistics & Probability Letters 80*(5-6), 386–389.

Foley, R. D. (1982). The non-homogeneous $M/G/\infty$ queue. *OpSearch 19*(1), 40–48.

Foote, B. L. (1976). A Queueing Case Study of Drive-In Banking. *Interfaces 6*(4), 31–37.

Foschini, G. and J. Salz (1978). A Basic Dynamic Routing Problem and Diffusion. *IEEE Transactions on Communications 26*(3), 320–327.

Galliher, H. P. and R. C. Wheeler (1958). Nonstationary Queuing Probabilities for Landing Congestion of Aircraft. *Operations Research 6*(2), 264–275.

Gans, N., G. Koole, and A. Mandelbaum (2003). Telephone Call Centers: Tutorial, Review, and Research Prospects. *Manufacturing & Service Operations Management 5*(2), 79–141.

Garnett, O. and A. Mandelbaum (2000). An Introduction to Skills-Based Routing and its Operational Complexities. Technical report, Technion - Israel Institute of Technology, Haifa.

Gaver, D. P. (1969). Highway Delays Resulting from Flow-Stopping Incidents. *Journal of Applied Probability 6*(1), 137–153.

Gillard, J. and V. Knight (2014). Using Singular Spectrum Analysis to obtain staffing level requirements in emergency units. *Journal of the Operational Research Society 65*(5), 735–746.

Giorno, V., A. G. Nobile, and L. M. Ricciardi (1987). On Some Time-Non-Homogeneous Diffusion Approximations to Queueing Systems. *Advances in Applied Probability 19*(4), 974–994.

Grassmann, W. (1977a). Transient solutions in Markovian queues - An algorithm for finding them and determining their waiting-time distributions. *European Journal of Operational Research 1*(6), 396–402.

Grassmann, W. K. (1977b). Transient solutions in markovian queueing systems. *Computers & Operations Research 4*(1), 47–53.

Green, L. and P. Kolesar (1991). The Pointwise Stationary Approximation for Queues with Nonstationary Arrivals. *Management Science 37*(1), 84–97.

Green, L., P. Kolesar, and A. Svoronos (1991). Some Effects of Non-stationarity on Multiserver Markovian Queueing Systems. *Operations Research 39*(3), 502–511.

Green, L. V. and P. J. Kolesar (1995). On the Accuracy of the Simple Peak Hour Approximation for Markovian Queues. *Management Science 41*(8), 1353–1370.

Green, L. V. and P. J. Kolesar (1997). The Lagged PSA for Estimating Peak Congestion in Multiserver Markovian Queues with Periodic Arrival Rates. *Management Science 43*(1), 80–87.

Green, L. V. and P. J. Kolesar (1998). A Note on Approximating Peak Congestion in $M_t/G/\infty$ Queues with Sinusoidal Arrivals. *Management Science 44*(11), S137–S144.

Green, L. V., P. J. Kolesar, and J. Soares (2001). Improving the SIPP Approach for Staffing Service Systems That Have Cyclic Demands. *Operations Research 49*(4), 549–564.

Green, L. V., P. J. Kolesar, and J. Soares (2003). An improved heuristic for staffing telephone call centers with limited operating hours. *Production and Operations Management 12*(1), 46–61.

Green, L. V., P. J. Kolesar, and W. Whitt (2007). Coping with Time-Varying Demand When Setting Staffing Requirements for a Service System. *Production and Operations Management 16*(1), 13–39.

Green, L. V. and J. Soares (2007). Computing Time-Dependent Waiting Time Probabilities in $M(t)/M/s(t)$ Queuing Systems. *Manufacturing & Service Operations Management 9*(1), 54–61.

Green, L. V., J. Soares, J. F. Giglio, and R. A. Green (2006). Using Queueing Theory to Increase the Effectiveness of Emergency Department Provider Staffing. *Academic emergency medicine 13*(1), 61–68.

Griffiths, J. D., W. Holland, and J. E. Williams (1991). Estimation of Queues at the Channel Tunnel. *Journal of the Operational Research Society 42*(5), 365–373.

Griffiths, J. D., G. M. Leonenko, and J. E. Williams (2008). Time-Dependent Analysis of Non-Empty $M/E_k/1$ Queue. *Quality Technology & Quantitative Managemen 5*(3), 309–320.

Gross, D. and D. R. Miller (1984). The Randomization Technique as a Modeling Tool and Solution Procedure for Transient Markov Processes. *Operations Research 32*(2), 343–361.

Hampshire, R. C., O. B. Jennings, and W. A. Massey (2009). A time-varying call center design via Lagrangian mechanics. *Probability in the Engineering and Informational Sciences 23*(2), 231–259.

Hampshire, R. C. and W. A. Massey (2010). Dynamic Optimization with Applications to Dynamic Rate Queues. In *Tutorials in Operations Research*, pp. 208–247. INFORMS.

Harrison, J. M. and A. Zeevi (2005). A Method for Staffing Large Call Centers Based on Stochastic Fluid Models. *Manufacturing & Service Operations Management 7*(1), 20–36.

Haughton, M. and K. P. S. Isotupa (2013). Flow control in capacity-constrained queueing systems with non-stationary arrivals. *Journal of the Operational Research Society 64*(2), 283–292.

Haughton, M. and K. P. Sapna Isotupa (2012). Scheduling commercial vehicle queues at a Canada-US border crossing. *Transportation Research Part E: Logistics and Transportation Review 48*(1), 190–201.

Hebert, J. E. and D. C. Dietz (1997). Modeling and Analysis of an Airport Departure Process. *Journal of Aircraft 34*(1), 43–47.

Holland, W. and J. D. Griffiths (1999). A time-dependent approximation for the queue $M/M(1, s)/c$. *IMA Journal of Mathematics Applied in Business & Industry 10*(3), 213–223.

Horonjeff, R. (1969). Analyses of Passenger and Baggage Flows in Airport Terminal Buildings. *Journal of Aircraft 6*(5), 446–451.

Ingolfsson, A., E. Akhmetshina, S. Budge, Y. Li, and X. Wu (2007). A Survey and Experimental Comparison of Service-Level-Approximation Methods for Nonstationary $M(t)/M/s(t)$ Queueing Systems with Exhaustive Discipline. *INFORMS Journal on Computing 19*(2), 201–214.

142

Ingolfsson, A., F. Campello, X. Wu, and E. Cabral (2010). Combining integer programming and the randomization method to schedule employees. *European Journal of Operational Research 202*(1), 153–163.

Ingolfsson, A., A. M. Haque, and A. Umnikov (2002). Accounting for time-varying queueing effects in workforce scheduling. *European Journal of Operational Research 139*(3), 585–597.

Jacquillat, A. and A. R. Odoni (2015). Endogenous control of service rates in stochastic and dynamic queuing models of airport congestion. *Transportation Research Part E: Logistics and Transportation Review 73*, 133–151.

Jagerman, D. L. (1975). Nonstationary Blocking in Telephone Traffic. *The Bell System Technical Journal 54*(3), 625–661.

Janic, M. (2005). Modelling Airport Congestion Charges. *Transportation Planning and Technology 28*(1), 1–26.

Janic, M. (2009). Modeling Airport Operations Affected by a Large-Scale Disruption. *Journal of Transportation Engineering 135*(4), 206–216.

Jennings, O. B., A. Mandelbaum, W. A. Massey, and W. Whitt (1996). Server Staffing to Meet Time-Varying Demand. *Management Science 42*(10), 1383–1394.

Jennings, O. B. and W. A. Massey (1997). A modified offered load approximation for nonstationary circuit switched networks. *Telecommunication Systems 7*(1-3), 229–251.

Jiménez, T. and G. Koole (2004). Scaling and comparison of fluid limits of queues applied to call centers with time-varying parameters. *OR Spectrum 26*(3), 413–422.

Jung, M. and E. S. Lee (1989a). A multi-echelon and multi-indenture repairable item queuing model during emergencies. *Mathematical and Computer Modelling 12*(7), 851–864.

Jung, M. and E. S. Lee (1989b). Numerical Optimization of a Queueing System by Dynamic Programming. *Journal of Mathematical Analysis and Applications 141*(1), 84–93.

Jung, W. (1993). Recoverable inventory systems with time-varying demand. *Production and Inventory Management Journal 34*(1), 77–81.

Kahraman, A. and A. Gosavi (2011). On the distribution of the number stranded in bulk-arrival, bulk-service queues of the $M/G/1$ form. *European Journal of Operational Research 212*(2), 352–360.

Kambo, N. S. and H. S. Bhalaik (1979). A note on the nonhomogeneous $M/M/\infty$ queue. *OpSearch 16*(2&3), 103–106.

Kasarda, J. D. and J. D. Green (2005). Air cargo as an economic development engine: A note on opportunities and constraints. *Journal of Air Transport Management 11*(6), 459–462.

Keller, J. B. (1982). Time-Dependent Queues. *SIAM Review 24*(4), 401–412.

Khintchine, A. Y. (1969). *Mathematical methods in the theory of queueing* (2nd ed.). London: Charles Griffin.

Kim, J. W. and S. H. Ha (2012). Advanced workforce management for effective customer services. *Quality & Quantity 46*(6), 1715–1726.

Kimber, R. M. and P. N. Daly (1986). Time-dependent queueing at road junctions: Observation and prediction. *Transportation Research Part B: Methodological 20*(3), 187–203.

Kimber, R. M. and E. M. Hollis (1978). Peak-period traffic delays at road junctions and other bottlenecks. *Traffic Engineering & Control 19*(10), 442–446.

Kimber, R. M., M. Marlow, and E. M. Hollis (1977). Flow/delay relationships for major/minor priority junctions. *Traffic Engineering & Control 18*(11), 516–519.

Kimura, T. (2004). Diffusion Models for Computer/Communication Systems. *Economic Journal of Hokkaido University 33*, 37–52.

Kleinrock, L. (1975). *Queueing Systems - Volume I: Theory*. New York: Wiley-Interscience.

Knessl, C. (2000). Exact and Asymptotic Solutions to a PDE That Arises in Time-Dependent Queues. *Advances in Applied Probability 32*(1), 256–283.

Knessl, C. and Y. Yang (2001). Analysis of a Brownian particle moving in a time-dependent drift field. *Asymptotic Analysis 27*(3-4), 281–319.

Knessl, C. and Y. P. Yang (2002). An Exact Solution for an $M(t)/M(t)/1$ Queue with Time-Dependent Arrivals and Service. *Queueing Systems 40*(3), 233–245.

Ko, Y. M. and N. Gautam (2010). Transient analysis of queues for peer-based multimedia content delivery. *IIE Transactions 42*(12), 881–896.

Ko, Y. M. and N. Gautam (2013). Critically Loaded Time-Varying Multiserver Queues: Computational Challenges and Approximations. *INFORMS Journal on Computing 25*(2), 285–301.

Kolesar, P. (1984). Stalking the Endangered CAT: A Queueing Analysis of Congestion at Automatic Teller Machines. *Interfaces 14*(6), 16–26.

Kolesar, P. J. and L. V. Green (1998). Insights on service system design from a normal approximation to Erlang's delay formula. *Production and Operations Management 7*(3), 282–293.

Kolesar, P. J., K. L. Rider, T. B. Crabill, and W. E. Walker (1975). A Queuing-Linear Programming Approach to Scheduling Police Patrol Cars. *Operations Research 23*(6), 1045–1062.

Kolmogorov, A. (1931). Sur le problème d' attente. *Matematicheskii Sbornik 38*(1-2), 101–106 (in French).

Koole, G. and A. Mandelbaum (2002). Queueing Models of Call Centers: An Introduction. *Annals of Operations Research 113*, 41–59.

Koole, G. and E. van der Sluis (2003). Optimal shift scheduling with a global service level constraint. *IIE Transactions 35*(11), 1049–1055.

Koopman, B. O. (1972). Air-Terminal Queues under Time-Dependent Conditions. *Operations Research 20*(6), 1089–1114.

Kuraya, K., H. Masuyama, and S. Kasahara (2011). Load distribution performance of super-node based peer-to-peer communication networks: A nonstationary Markov chain approach. *Numerical Algebra, Control and Optimization 1*(4), 593–610.

Kuraya, K., H. Masuyama, S. Kasahara, and Y. Takahashi (2009). Decentralized user information management systems for peer-to-peer communication networks: An approach by nonstationary peer-population process. *Ubiquitous Computing and Communication Journal CSNDSP2008*, 1–8.

Kuwahara, M. (2007). A theory and implications on dynamic marginal cost. *Transportation Research Part A: Policy and Practice 41*(7), 627–643.

Kwan, S. K., M. M. Davis, and A. G. Greenwood (1988). A simulation model for determining variable worker requirements in a service operation with time-dependent customer demand. *Queueing Systems 3*(3), 265–275.

Lackman, R. A., J. D. Spragins, and D. Tipper (1992). Scheduling real-time and non-real-time traffic under nonstationary conditions. *Annals of Operations Research 36*(1), 193–224.

Lau, H. C. and H. Song (2008). Multi-echelon repairable item inventory system with limited repair capacity under nonstationary demands. *International Journal of Inventory Research 1*(1), 67–92.

Lee, C., H. C. Huang, B. Liu, and Z. Xu (2006). Development of timed Colour Petri net simulation models for air cargo terminal operations. *Computers & Industrial Engineering 51*(1), 102–110.

Leese, E. L. and D. W. Boyd (1966). Numerical methods of determining the transient behaviour of queues with variable arrival rates. *Journal of the Canadian Operational Research Society 4*(1), 1–13.

Leleu, C. and D. Marsh (2009). Dependent on the Dark: Cargo and Other Night Flights in European Airspace. Trends in Air Traffic 5. Brussels: EUROCONTROL.

Liu, Y. and L. M. Wein (2008). A Queueing Analysis to Determine How Many Additional Beds Are Needed for the Detention and Removal of Illegal Aliens. *Management Science 54*(1), 1–15.

Liu, Y. and W. Whitt (2011). Large-time asymptotics for the $G_t/M_t/s_t + GI_t$ many-server fluid queue with abandonment. *Queueing Systems 67*(2), 145–182.

Liu, Y. and W. Whitt (2012a). Stabilizing Customer Abandonment in Many-Server Queues with Time-Varying Arrivals. *Operations Research 60*(6), 1551–1564.

Liu, Y. and W. Whitt (2012b). The $G_t/GI/s_t + GI$ many-server fluid queue. *Queueing Systems 71*(4), 405–444.

Liu, Y. and W. Whitt (2014). Many-server heavy-traffic limit for queues with time-varying parameters. *The Annals of Applied Probability 24*(1), 378–421.

Liu, Z. and R. Righter (1998). Optimal Load Balancing on Distributed Homogeneous Unreliable Processors. *Operations Research 46*(4), 563–573.

Lovell, D. J., K. Vlachou, T. Rabbani, and A. Bayen (2013). A diffusion approximation to a single airport queue. *Transportation Research Part C: Emerging Technologies 33*, 227–237.

Luchak, G. (1956). The Solution of the Single-Channel Queuing Equations Characterized by a Time-Dependent Poisson-Distributed Arrival Rate and a General Class of Holding Times. *Operations Research 4(6)*, 711–732.

Luchak, G. (1957). The Distribution of the Time Required to Reduce to Some Preassigned Level a Single-Channel Queue Characterized by a Time-Dependent Poisson-Distributed Arrival Rate and a General Class of Holding Times. *Operations Research 5(2)*, 205–209.

Lyubarskii, G. Y. (1982). Busy time of a nonstationary single-channel service system and related questions. *Automation and Remote Control 43(12)*, 1537–1543.

Mandelbaum, A. and W. A. Massey (1995). Strong Approximations for Time-Dependent Queues. *Mathematics of Operations Research 20(1)*, 33–64.

Mandelbaum, A., W. A. Massey, and M. I. Reiman (1998). Strong approximations for Markovian service networks. *Queueing Systems 30(1-2)*, 149–201.

Mandelbaum, A., W. A. Massey, M. I. Reiman, A. Stolyar, and B. Rider (2002). Queue Lengths and Waiting Times for Multiserver Queues with Abandonment and Retrials. *Telecommunication Systems 21(2-4)*, 149–171.

Mandelbaum, A. and S. Zeltyn (2004). The impact of customers' patience on delay and abandonment: some empirically-driven experiments with the $M/M/n + G$ queue. *OR Spectrum 26(3)*, 377–411.

Manohar, P., S. S. Ram, and D. Manjunath (2009). Path Coverage by a Sensor Field: The Nonhomogeneous Case. *ACM Transactions on Sensor Networks 5*(2), 1–26.

Margolius, B. H. (1999). A sample path analysis of the $M_t/M_t/c$ queue. *Queueing systems 31*(1-2), 59–93.

Margolius, B. H. (2005). Transient Solution to the Time-Dependent Multiserver Poisson Queue. *Journal of Applied Probability 42*(3), 766–777.

Margolius, B. H. (2007). Transient and periodic solution to the time-inhomogeneous quasi-birth death process. *Queueing Systems 56*(3-4), 183–194.

Margolius, B. H. (2008). The matrices R and G of matrix analytic methods and the time-inhomogeneous periodic Quasi-Birth-and-Death process. *Queueing Systems 60*(1-2), 131–151.

Massey, W. A. (1985). Asymptotic analysis of the time dependent $M/M/1$ queue. *Mathematics of Operations Research 10*(2), 305–327.

Massey, W. A. (2002). The Analysis of Queues with Time-Varying Rates for Telecommunication Models. *Telecommunication Systems 21*(2-4), 173–204.

Massey, W. A. and J. Pender (2013). Gaussian skewness approximation for dynamic rate multi-server queues with abandonment. *Queueing Systems 75*(2-4), 243–277.

Massey, W. A. and W. Whitt (1997). Peak congestion in multi-server service systems with slowly varying arrival rates. *Queueing Systems 25*(1-4), 157–172.

McCalla, C. and W. Whitt (2002). A Time-Dependent Queueing-Network Model to Describe the Life-Cycle Dynamics of Private-Line Telecommunication Services. *Telecommunication Systems 19*(1), 9–38.

Mejía-Téllez, J. and D. Worthington (1994). Practical methods for queue length behaviour for bulk service queues of the form $M/G^{0,C}/1$ and $M(t)/G^{0,C}/1$. *European Journal of Operational Research 73*(1), 103–113.

Minh, D. L. (1978). The Discrete-Time Single-Server Queue with Time-Inhomogeneous Compound Poisson Input and General Service Time Distribution. *Journal of Applied Probability 15*(3), 590–601.

Mok, S. K. and J. G. Shanthikumar (1987). A transient queueing model for Business Office with standby servers. *European Journal of Operational Research 28*(2), 158–174.

Moore, S. C. (1975). Approximating the Behavior of Nonstationary Single-Server Queues. *Operations Research 23*(5), 1011–1032.

Nasr, W. W. and M. R. Taaffe (2013). Fitting the $Ph_t/M_t/s/c$ Time-Dependent Departure Process for Use in Tandem Queueing Networks. *INFORMS Journal on Computing 25*(4), 758–773.

Nelson, B. L. and M. R. Taaffe (2004). The $Ph_t/Ph_t/\infty$ Queueing System: Part I-The Single Node. *INFORMS Journal on Computing 16*(3), 266–274.

Newell, G. F. (1966). The $M/G/\infty$ Queue. *SIAM Journal on Applied Mathematics 14*(1), 86–88.

Newell, G. F. (1968a). Queues with Time-Dependent Arrival Rates I - The Transition through Saturation. *Journal of Applied Probability 5*(2), 436–451.

Newell, G. F. (1968b). Queues with Time-Dependent Arrival Rates: II - The Maximum Queue and the Return to Equilibrium. *Journal of Applied Probability 5*(3), 579–590.

Newell, G. F. (1968c). Queues with Time-Dependent Arrival Rates III - A Mild Rush Hour. *Journal of Applied Probability 5*(3), 591–606.

Newell, G. F. (1971). *Applications of Queueing Theory*. London: Chapman and Hall.

Newell, G. F. (1979). Airport Capacity and Delays. *Transportation Science 13*(3), 201–241.

Nozari, A. (1985). Control of Entry to a Nonstationary Queuing System. *Naval Research Logistics Quarterly 32*(2), 275–286.

Odoni, A. R. and E. Roth (1983). An Empirical Investigation of the Transient Behavior of Stationary Queueing Systems. *Operations Research 31*(3), 432–455.

Omosigho, S. E. and D. J. Worthington (1985). The single server queue with inhomogeneous arrival rate and discrete service time distribution. *European Journal of Operational Research 22*(3), 397–407.

Omosigho, S. E. and D. J. Worthington (1988). An approximation of known accuracy for single server queues with inhomogeneous arrival rate and continuous service time distribution. *European Journal of Operational Research 33*(3), 304–313.

Ong, K. L. and M. R. Taaffe (1988). Approximating nonstationary $Ph(t)/Ph(t)/1/c$ queueing systems. *Mathematics and Computers in Simulation 30*(5), 441–452.

Ou, J., V. N. Hsu, and C.-L. Li (2010). Scheduling Truck Arrivals at an Air Cargo Terminal. *Production and Operations Management 19*(1), 83–97.

Ou, J., H. Zhou, and Z. Li (2007). A Simulation Study of Logistics Operations at an Air Cargo Terminal. In *Proceedings of the 2007 International Conference on Wireless Communications, Networking and Mobile Computing*, pp. 4403–4407.

Palm, C. (1943). *Intensitätsschwankungen im Fernsprechverkehr - Unter-suchungen über die Darstellung auf Fernsprechverkehrsprobleme an-wendbarer stochastischer Prozesse*. Stockholm: Ericsson Technics.

Pang, G. and W. Whitt (2012a). Infinite-server queues with batch arrivals and dependent service times. *Probability in the Engineering and Informational Sciences 26*(2), 197–220.

Pang, G. and W. Whitt (2012b). The Impact of Dependent Service Times on Large-Scale Service Systems. *Manufacturing & Service Operations Management 14*(2), 262–278.

Parlar, M. (1984). Optimal dynamic service rate control in time dependent $M/M/S/N$ queues. *International Journal of Systems Science 15*(1), 107–118.

Parthasarathy, P. R. and R. Sudhesh (2006). An exact solution for an $M/M/1$ queue with piecewise-constant rates. *The Mathematical Scientist 31*(1), 48–52.

Paullin, R. L. and R. Horonjeff (1969). Sizing of departure lounges in airport buildings. *Transportation Engineering Journal of ASCE 95*(2), 267–277.

Pender, J. (2014a). A Poisson-Charlier approximation for nonstationary queues. *Operations Research Letters 42*(4), 293–298.

Pender, J. (2014b). Gram charlier expansion for time varying multi-server queues with abandonment. *SIAM Journal on Applied Mathematics 74*(4), 1238–1265.

Powell, W. B. and H. P. Simão (1986). Numerical simulation of transient bulk queues with general vehicle dispatching strategies. *Transportation Research Part B: Methodological 20*(6), 477–490.

Purdue, P. (1974a). Stochastic theory of compartments. *Bulletin of Mathematical Biology 36*(3), 305–309.

Purdue, P. (1974b). Stochastic theory of compartments: One and two compartment systems. *Bulletin of Mathematical Biology 36*(5-6), 577–587.

Ramakrishnan, C. S. (1980). A note on the $M/D/\infty$ queue. *OpSearch 17*(2&3), 118.

Rider, K. L. (1976). A Simple Approximation to the Average Queue Size in the Time-Dependent $M/M/1$ Queue. *Journal of the ACM 23*(2), 361–367.

Ridley, A. D., W. Massey, and M. Fu (2004). Fluid Approximation of a Priority Call Center With Time-Varying Arrivals. *Telecommunications Review 15*, 69–77.

Rong, A. and M. Grunow (2009). Shift designs for freight handling personnel at air cargo terminals. *Transportation Research Part E: Logistics and Transportation Review 45*(5), 725–739.

Rosenlund, S. I. (1976). Busy Periods in Time-Dependent $M/G/1$ Queues. *Advances in Applied Probability 8*(1), 195–208.

Ross, K. W. and D. D. Yao (1991). Optimal load balancing and scheduling in a distributed computer system. *Journal of the ACM 38*(3), 676–690.

Rothkopf, M. H. and R. G. Johnston (1982). Routine Analysis of Periodic Queues. *IIE Transactions 14*(3), 214–218.

Rothkopf, M. H. and S. S. Oren (1979). A Closure Approximation for the Nonstationary $M/M/s$ Queue. *Management Science 25*(6), 522–534.

Schwartz, B. L. (1974). Queuing Models with Lane Selection: A New Class of Problems. *Operations Research 22*(2), 331–339.

Schwarz, J. A., G. Selinka, and R. Stolletz (2016). Performance analysis of time-dependent queueing systems: survey and classification. *Omega 63*, 170–189.

Selinka, G., A. Franz, and R. Stolletz (2016). Time-dependent Performance Approximation of Truck Handling Operations at an Air Cargo Terminal. *Computers & Operations Research 65*, 164–173.

Shanbhag, D. N. (1966). On Infinite Server Queues with Batch Arrivals. *Journal of Applied Probability 3*(1), 274–279.

Sharma, O. P. and U. C. Gupta (1983). $M/M/\infty$ Queues in series with non-homogeneous inputs. *Mathematische Operationsforschung und Statistik. Series Optimization 14*(3), 445–453.

Singer, M. and P. Donoso (2008). Assessing an ambulance service with queuing theory. *Computers & Operations Research 35*(8), 2549–2560.

Stadje, W. (1990). A note on the simple queue with variable intensities and two servers. *Operations Research Letters 9*(1), 45–49.

Steckley, S. G. and S. G. Henderson (2007). The error in steady-state approximations for the time-dependent waiting time distribution. *Stochastic Models 23*(2), 307–332.

Stolletz, R. (2008a). Approximation of the non-stationary $M(t)/M(t)/c(t)$-queue using stationary queueing models: The stationary backlog-carryover approach. *European Journal of Operational Research 190*(2), 478–493.

Stolletz, R. (2008b). Non-stationary delay analysis of runway systems. *OR Spectrum 30*(1), 191–213.

Stolletz, R. (2011). Analysis of passenger queues at airport terminals. *Research in Transportation Business & Management 1*(1), 144–149.

Stolletz, R. and S. Lagershausen (2013). Time-dependent performance evaluation for loss-waiting queues with arbitrary distributions. *International Journal of Production Research 51*(5), 1366–1378.

Swaroop, P., B. Zou, M. O. Ball, and M. Hansen (2012). Do more US airports need slot controls? A welfare based approach to determine slot levels. *Transportation Research Part B: Methodological 46*(9), 1239–1259.

Sze, D. Y. (1984). A Queueing Model for Telephone Operator Staffing. *Operations Research 32*(2), 229–249.

Taaffe, M. R. and G. M. Clark (1988). Approximating Nonstationary Two-Priority Non-Preemptive Queueing Systems. *Naval Research Logistics 35*(1), 125–145.

Taaffe, M. R. and K. L. Ong (1987). Approximating nonstationary $Ph(t)/M(t)/s/c$ queueing systems. *Annals of Operations Research 8*(1), 103–116.

Tan, X., C. Knessl, and Y. P. Yang (2013). On finite capacity queues with time dependent arrival rates. *Stochastic Processes and their Applications 123*(6), 2175–2227.

Tarabia, A. M. K. (2000). Transient Analysis of $M/M/1/N$ Queue - An Alternative Approach. *Tamkang Journal of Science and Engineering 3*(4), 263–266.

Technion (2000). Call center data, Technion, Israel Institute of Technology. *Downloadable at http://ie.technion.ac.il/serveng/callcenterdata/s.*

Teh, Y.-C. and A. R. Ward (2002). Critical Thresholds for Dynamic Routing in Queueing Networks. *Queueing Systems 42*(3), 297–316.

Thakur, A. K. and A. Rescigno (1978). On the stochastic theory of compartments: III. General time-dependent reversible systems. *Bulletin of Mathematical Biology 40*(2), 237–246.

Thakur, A. K., A. Rescigno, and D. E. Schafer (1972). On the stochastic theory of compartments: I. A single-compartment system. *The Bulletin of Mathematical Biophysics 34*(1), 53–63.

Thompson, G. M. (1993). Accounting for the multi-period impact of service when determining employee requirements for labor scheduling. *Journal of Operations Management 11*(3), 269–287.

Tipper, D. and M. K. Sundareshan (1990). Numerical Methods for Modeling Computer Networks Under Nonstationary Conditions. *IEEE Journal on Selected Areas in Communications 8*(9), 1682–1695.

Tošić, V. (1992). A review of airport passenger terminal operations analysis and modelling. *Transportation Research Part A: Policy and Practice 26*(1), 3–26.

Tripathi, S. K. and A. Duda (1986). Time-dependent analysis of queueing systems. *INFOR 24*(3), 199–220.

Upton, R. A. and S. K. Tripathi (1982). An Approximate Transient Analysis of the $M(t)/M/1$ Queue. *Performance Evaluation 2*(2), 118–132.

Van As, H. R. (1986). Transient Analysis of Markovian Queueing Systems and Its Application to Congestion-Control Modeling. *IEEE Journal on Selected Areas in Communications 4*(6), 891–904.

Van de Coevering, M. C. T. (1995). Computing transient performance measures for the $M/M/1$ queue. *OR Spektrum 17*, 19–22.

Van Dijk, N. M. (1992). Uniformization for nonhomogeneous Markov chains. *Operations Research Letters 12*(5), 283–291.

Vanberkel, P. T., R. J. Boucherie, E. W. Hans, and J. L. Hurink (2014). Optimizing the strategic patient mix combining queueing theory and dynamic programming. *Computers & Operations Research 43*, 271–279.

Viti, F. and H. J. van Zuylen (2009). The Dynamics and the Uncertainty of Queues at Fixed and Actuated Controls: A Probabilistic Approach. *Journal of Intelligent Transportation Systems 13*(1), 39–51.

Viti, F. and H. J. van Zuylen (2010). Probabilistic models for queues at fixed control signals. *Transportation Research Part B: Methodological 44*(1), 120–135.

Wall, A. D. and D. J. Worthington (2007). Time-dependent analysis of virtual waiting time behaviour in discrete time queues. *European Journal of Operational Research 178*(2), 482–499.

Wan, Y.-w., R. K. Cheung, J. Liu, and J. H. Tong (1998). Warehouse location problems for air freight forwarders: a challenge created by the airport relocation. *Journal of Air Transport Management 4*(4), 201–207.

Wang, W.-P., D. Tipper, and S. Banerjee (1996). A Simple Approximation for Modeling Nonstationary Queues. In *Proceedings of IEEE INFO-COM'96. Conference on Computer Communications*, pp. 255–262.

Whitt, W. (1991). The Pointwise Stationary Approximation for $M_t/M_t/s$ Queues is Asymptotically Correct As the Rates Increase. *Management Science 37*(3), 307–314.

Whitt, W. (1999). Using different response-time requirements to smooth time-varying demand for service. *Operations Research Letters 24*(1-2), 1–10.

Whitt, W. (2007). What You Should Know About Queueing Models to Set Staffing Requirements in Service Systems. *Naval Research Logistics 54*(5), 476–484.

Whitt, W. (2013). OM Forum - Offered Load Analysis for Staffing. *Manufacturing & Service Operations Management 15*(2), 166–169.

Wirasinghe, S. C. and S. Bandara (1990). Airport gate position estimation for minimum total costs -Approximate closed form solution. *Transportation Research Part B: Methodological 24*(4), 287–297.

Wirasinghe, S. C. and M. Shehata (1988). Departure lounge sizing and optimal seating capacity for a given aircraft/flight mix - (i) single gate. (ii) several gates. *Transportation Planning and Technology 13*(1), 57–71.

Worthington, D. and A. Wall (1999). Using the discrete time modelling approach to evaluate the time-dependent behaviour of queueing systems. *Journal of the Operational Research Society 50*(8), 777–788.

Wragg, A. (1963). The solution of an infinite set of differential-difference equations occurring in polymerization and queueing problems. *Mathematical Proceedings of the Cambridge Philosophical Society 59*(01), 117–124.

Xu, K., D. Tipper, Y. Qian, P. Krishnamurthy, and S. Tipmongkonsilp (2014). Time-Varying Performance Analysis of Multihop Wireless Networks with CBR Traffic. *IEEE Transactions on Vehicular Technology in Press.*

Yang, Y. and C. Knessl (1997). Asymptotic analysis of the $M/G/1$ queue with a time-dependent arrival rate. *Queueing Systems 26*(1-2), 23–68.

Yang, Z.-Z., G. Chen, and D.-P. Song (2013). Integrating truck arrival management into tactical operation planning at container terminals. *Polish Maritime Research 20*(Special Issue), 32–46.

Yin, G. and H. Zhang (2002). Countable-State-Space Markov Chains with Two Time Scales and Applications to Queueing Systems. *Advances in Applied Probability 34*(3), 662–688.

Yom-Tov, G. B. and A. Mandelbaum (2014). Erlang-R: A Time-Varying Queue with Reentrant Customers, in Support of Healthcare Staffing. *Manufacturing & Service Operations Management 16*(2), 283–299.

Zeltyn, S. and A. Mandelbaum (2005). Call Centers with Impatient Customers: Many-Server Asymptotics of the $M/M/n+G$ Queue. *Queueing Systems 51*(3-4), 361–402.

Zhang, J. and E. J. Coyle (1991). The Transient Solution of Time-Dependent $M/M/1$ Queues. *IEEE Transactions on Information Theory 37*(6), 1690–1696.

Zhang, Z. G. (2009). Performance Analysis of a Queue with Congestion-Based Staffing Policy. *Management Science 55*(2), 240–251.

Curriculum vitae

Gregor Selinka

Personal Information

Name	Gregor Selinka
Date of birth	01.03.1983
Place of birth	Tübingen
Nationality	German

Education

Since 01/2011	*Doctoral Candidate* Chair of Production Management, Business School, University of Mannheim
10/2004 - 06/2010	Diploma in Industrial Engineering and Management Karlsruhe Institute of Technology (KIT)
10/2002 - 07/2004	Studies in Aerospace Engineering University of Stuttgart
07/2002	Abitur, Johannes-Kepler-Gymnasium, Reutlingen

Professional Experience

Since 01/2016	*Consultant* CC Integrated Business Planning, Camelot Management Consultants AG, Mannheim

01/2011 - 12/2015	*Research Assistant*
	Chair of Production Management,
	Business School, University of Mannheim
04/2008 - 09/2008	*Internship*
	Transportation and Network Management,
	Lufthansa Technik Logistik GmbH (LTL), Hamburg
08/2006 - 02/2008,	*Student Assistant*
10/2008 - 12/2010	Competence Center Industrial and Service Innovations,
	Fraunhofer Institute for Systems and Innovation Research ISI, Karlsruhe